The Fight Renewed:
The Civil Rights Movement

Lucent Library of Black History

Adam Woog

LUCENT BOOKS

An imprint of Thomson Gale, a part of The Thomson Corporation

THOMSON
★
GALE

Detroit • New York • San Francisco • San Diego • New Haven, Conn.
Waterville, Maine • London • Munich

For my father, Alan Woog, and Coretta Scott King, in honor of their long friendship
and for Rita Schwerener Bender, with gratitude for helping Karen and I complete our family.

For more information, contact
Lucent Books
27500 Drake Rd.
Farmington Hills, MI 48331-3535
Or you can visit our Internet site at http://www.gale.com

LIBRARY OF CONGRESS CATALOGING-IN-PUBLICATION DATA

Woog, Adam, 1953–
    The fight renewed : the civil rights movement / by Adam Woog.
        p. cm. — (The Lucent library of Black history)
Includes bibliographical references and index.
ISBN 1-59018-701-6 (hardcover : alk. paper)
1. African Americans—Civil rights—History—20th century—Juvenile literature. 2. Civil
rights movements—United States—History—20th century—Juvenile literature. 3.
United States—Race relations—Juvenile literature. I. Title. II. Series.
E185.61.W926 2005
323.1196'073—dc22
                                                                                2005001662

Printed in the United States of America

Contents

Foreword

It has been more than five hundred years since Africans were first brought to the New World in shackles, and over 140 years since slavery was formally abolished in the United States. Over fifty years have passed since the fallacy of "separate but equal" was obliterated in the American courts, and some forty years since the watershed Civil Rights Act of 1965 guaranteed the rights and liberties of all Americans, especially those of color. Over time, these changes have become celebrated landmarks in American history. In the twenty-first century, African American men and women are politicians, judges, diplomats, professors, deans, doctors, artists, athletes, business owners, and home owners. For many, the scars of the past have melted away in the opportunities that have been found in contemporary society. Observers such as Peter N. Kirsanow, who sits on the U.S. Commission of Civil Rights, point to these accomplishments and conclude, "The growing black middle class may be viewed as proof that most of the civil rights battles have been won."

In spite of these legal victories, however, prejudice and inequality have persisted in American society. In 2003, African Americans comprised just 12 percent of the nation's population, yet accounted for 44 percent of its prison inmates and 24 percent of its poor. Racially motivated hate crimes continue to appear on the pages of major newspapers in many American cities. Furthermore, many African Americans still experience either overt or muted racism in their daily lives. A 1996 study undertaken by Professor Nancy Krieger of the Harvard School of Public Health, for example, found that 80 percent of the African American participants reported having experienced racial discrimination in one or more settings, including at work or school, applying for housing and medical care, from the police or in the courts, and on the street or in a public setting.

It is for these reasons that many believe the struggle for racial equality and justice is far from over. These episodes of discrimination threaten to shatter the illusion that America has complete-ly overcome its racist past, causing many black Americans to become increasingly frustrated and confused. Scholar and writer Ellis Cose has described this splintered state in the following way: "I have done everything I was supposed to do. I have stayed out of trouble with the law, gone to the right schools, and worked myself nearly to death. What more do they want? Why in God's name won't they accept me as a full human being?" For Cose and others, the struggle for equality and justice has yet to be fully achieved.

In many subtle yet important ways, the traumatic experiences of slavery and segregation continue to inform the way race is dis-cussed and experienced in the twenty-first century. Indeed, it is possible that America will always grapple with the fallout from its distressing past. Ulric Haynes, dean of the Hofstra University School of Business has said, "Perhaps race will always matter, given the historical circumstances under which we came to this country." But studying this past and understanding how it con-tributes to present-day dialogues about race and history in Amer-ica is a critical component of contemporary education. To this end, the Lucent Library of Black History offers a thorough look at the experiences that have shaped the black community and the American people as a whole. Annotated bibliographies provide readers with ideas for further research, while fully documented primary and secondary source quotations enhance the text. Each book in the series explores a different episode of black history; together they provide students with a wealth of information as well as launching points for further study and discussion.

Introduction

We Shall Overcome

The issue of race relations has always been one of the most divisive and dramatic social conflicts in American history. It began well before the United States became a nation, and it continues today. This troubled history is closely linked to the issue of civil rights, the fundamental freedoms guaranteed to citizens, such as the rights of freedom of speech and religion and equal protection under the law. In America such rights are enshrined in the Constitution's Bill of Rights and enforced by a body of legislation.

The democratic principles of civil rights theoretically apply to all Americans, including minorities. However, for African Americans, the country's largest minority group, the reality has been far different. For centuries, black Americans were denied even the most basic rights, and in some ways they are still fighting for full equality. A distinguished civil rights attorney, Charles Houston, once commented, "Nobody needs to explain to a Negro the difference between the law in books and the law in action."[1]

Centuries of Inequality

The heart-wrenching history of racial discrimination, and the struggle to give black Americans genuine equality, is rooted in the colonial era. From the first settlements of the early 1600s, and for nearly a century after the United States declared independence, blacks were held in slavery in several states and both socially and legally considered barely human. Even after gaining their freedom following the Civil War, African Americans were still treated as second-class citizens.

Blacks and whites lived segregated lives, especially in the South. They went to separate schools, lived in separate neighborhoods, and often had separate public facilities such as theaters, stadiums, transportation, restrooms, and restaurants. Their lives were not only segregated but unequal, since services and facilities

A black man and a white child drink from segregated water fountains in South Carolina. From the end of the Civil War, segregated facilities were the norm in the South.

available to blacks—especially in the South—were typically poor and inadequate. This situation, however, changed significantly in the mid-twentieth century, in response to the modern civil rights movement.

The Civil Rights Movement Begins

The pivotal events of the civil rights movement occurred in a single decade, from the mid-1950s to the mid-1960s. However, organized protests concerning African American rights long predated and followed these years. It is difficult to determine the exact start of the movement. Some authorities believe that it was President Harry Truman's complete desegregation of the military after World War II. Others point to the Supreme Court decision of *Brown v. Board of Education* in 1954, which struck down the long-held concept of "separate but equal" schools. Still others argue that the movement truly began with the Montgomery bus boycott of 1955–1956, the first large-scale protest of the period. All of these events were important milestones in a growing, coalescing surge of emotion and activism.

Martin Luther King Jr. rides a Montgomery, Alabama, bus in 1956. Some historians date the beginning of the Civil Rights Movement to the Montgomery bus boycott of 1955-1956.

Many people played key roles in this blossoming movement—not only high-profile leaders but countless numbers of anonymous yet brave and tireless activists. Nonetheless, one man was, and still is, most closely associated with the fight for civil rights. This was a young, charismatic Baptist minister named Dr. Martin Luther King Jr.

King's leadership was based on the doctrine of nonviolence. This philosophy was based, in large part, on his deeply held belief in Christian love and compassion, which avoided answering violence with violence. Although the push for civil rights attracted supporters from many religions and walks of life, the movement was always deeply rooted in this Christian concept of "turning the other cheek" to one's attackers. It is no coincidence that many other civil rights leaders were ministers like King or that churches were frequently key meeting grounds for movement organizers.

Wedded to the Christian doctrine of love and compassion was the concept of civil disobedience—that is, protests that deliberately and nonviolently disobeyed unjust laws. Such tactics were not invented during the American civil rights movement; the Indian political and spiritual leader Mohandas (Mahatma) Gandhi pioneered them in the 1920s. Gandhi was largely credited with achieving Indian independence from Great Britain after World War II, not through armed rebellion but by using civil disobedience to force political change.

Gandhi's ideas resonated strongly with King. The Baptist preacher recognized that nonviolence was an effective, dramatic means of focusing public attention on injustices, forcing change in situations that might otherwise be ignored. As the movement gathered energy King noted, "We have gained a new sense of dignity and destiny. We have discovered a new and powerful weapon—non-violent resistance."[2]

"Too Great a Burden"

Opponents of the civil rights movement did not adhere to the same principles of nonviolence. Especially in the South, the movement was met with frequent violence by civilian vigilantes, police, and other officials. Often, authorities looked the other way when racist groups such as the notorious Ku Klux Klan attacked nonviolent protesters.

"Crops Without Plowing"

The civil rights movement required struggle and confrontation as well as personal initiative, sacrifice, and courage. The distinguished civil rights pioneer Frederick Douglass recognized this in 1857 when he said (in a passage reprinted in William Yeingst's article "Sitting for Justice"), "Those who profess to favor freedom and yet deprecate agitation are men who want crops without plowing the ground. They want rain without thunder and lightning. They want the ocean without the awful roar of its waters. Power concedes nothing without a demand. It never did, and it never will."

The history of the civil rights movement is thus shot through with incident after violent incident: beatings, bombings, intimidation, house burnings, and even murder. For years, civil rights activists did not succumb to the temptation to meet this violence with violence of their own. Martin Luther King once said, "I've seen too much hate to want to hate myself; hate is too great a burden to bear."[3]

However, by the late 1960s the era of nonviolent protest was passing, overshadowed by angry black activists who took a more militant stance. Protests became more confrontational, and the period was marked by riots and bloody demonstrations. King himself became a victim of the escalating violence when he was assassinated in 1968.

To many observers, King's death was a devastating blow that marked the end of the civil rights movement, or at least the beginning of the end. Others, however, feel that the era never truly ended. Myrlie Evers, the widow of Medgar Evers, a prominent civil rights worker who was murdered in 1963, comments, "We're still fighting for first-class citizenship."[4] To such activists, the fight for equality continues to this day, in such forms as programs fostering jobs for minorities and educational equality.

However the period is defined, the roots of the civil rights movement reach back hundreds of years. Its story begins even before America became a country.

Chapter One

The Roots of the Civil Rights Movement

No one knows exactly how many black people were part of the barbaric slave trade between Africa and the seventeenth-century European colonies in the Caribbean and North America. Total estimates vary from 10 million to 100 million.

Only a small percentage, perhaps 10 percent of the slave population, lived in the British colonies that later became the United States. The first recorded slaves in these colonies arrived in 1619. By 1750 there were about 200,000, mostly in the South, where massive numbers of manual laborers were needed to produce such labor-intensive crops as rice, tobacco, sugarcane, and, later, cotton.

"Naturally Inferior"

After the colonies achieved independence, slavery developed regionally in America. By the mid-1800s, all of the northern states had abolished the practice. However, slavery continued to be an accepted part of life in the South, and by 1860 some 4 million slaves toiled there.

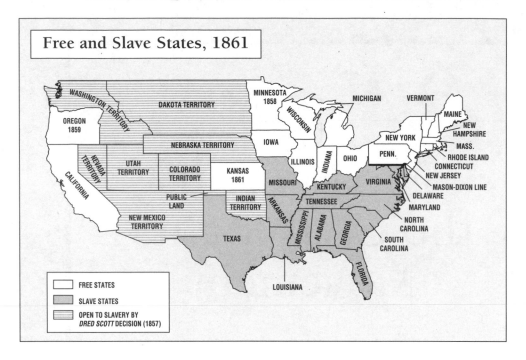

Free and Slave States, 1861

FREE STATES
SLAVE STATES
OPEN TO SLAVERY BY *DRED SCOTT* DECISION (1857)

Slaves were considered property, with no more rights than a cow or a horse. Their owners were free to buy and sell them; they lived in often deplorable conditions; and many were routinely subject to terrible cruelty and degradation, frequently beaten, raped, or separated from their families. In some cases, masters could kill their slaves without punishment, because the destruction of one's own property was legally no one else's business.

To lessen the chances of a revolt, slaves were forbidden to possess weapons or meet with other slaves. They could not testify against white people in court, and they typically received far harsher punishments for crimes than whites. Nor were they able to receive an education; in some regions, it was illegal to teach a slave to read.

Southern whites had little trouble justifying the practice of slavery. Their belief—bolstered by religious scriptures and pseudoscientific claims—was that whites were inherently superior in intelligence, talent, and moral standards. The Scottish philosopher David Hume was typical of many when he wrote in 1748, "I am apt to suspect the Negroes and in general all the other species of men to be naturally inferior to the whites. There never was a civilized nation of any other complexion than white."[5]

Freedom of Sorts

The general attitude was different in the North. Most northerners were indifferent to slavery, and a few passionately opposed it. Even in the North, however, "free Negroes" did not have easy lives. Being free was not the same as being equal.

Blacks were still not citizens in northern states, and thus were denied such basic rights as voting. Also, many northern whites refused to mingle, so the races remained mostly segregated. The best hotels, restaurants, theaters, and other public places were off-limits to blacks; those that did cater to them were shabby and inferior. Education for free blacks was a rarity, and usually only the most menial jobs were available to them.

Nonetheless, freedom in the North was clearly superior to slavery in the South. If possible, slaves saved money to buy their freedom and head north. This was difficult, however. A few desperate slaves attempted organized rebellion. One such rebellious slave was Nat Turner, a deeply religious Virginian. In 1831 Turner experienced a series of visions that told him that "I should arise and prepare myself and slay my enemies with their own weapons."[6] He led others in a revolt that resulted in the deaths of over fifty whites before he was captured and hanged.

Other slaves tried to escape to the North or Canada. The most common way was through a secret network of supporters known as the Underground Railroad. Free blacks and sympathetic whites provided escapees with food, shelter, transportation, and clothing during these dangerous journeys. One such hero was Harriet Tubman, who was born a slave but found her freedom in the North. Tubman risked certain death by returning to the South some nineteen times, leading at least three hundred slaves to freedom.

Scott, Stowe, and Brown

A handful of blacks tried to take legal action to gain their freedom, paving the way for legal victories that came later. One such pioneer was Dred Scott, a slave who sued to gain his freedom. Scott argued that he became free when he traveled with his owner from his home in the slave state of Missouri to the free states of Illinois and Minnesota.

In 1852 the Missouri Supreme Court ruled against him. It decided that Scott had become a slave again when he reentered

Missouri. The case was then argued before the U.S. Supreme Court, which again decided against Scott. The Court ruled that no black person, free or enslaved, could be an American citizen; therefore, no black person had the right to sue in federal court, so Scott's argument was nullified.

Meanwhile, a number of northern whites worked tirelessly to abolish slavery everywhere in America. Some gave speeches and expressed their opinions in a variety of publications. One particularly influential book was Harriet Beecher Stowe's novel *Uncle Tom's Cabin*, a best seller from 1852 that poignantly highlighted the plight of slaves.

A few zealous abolitionists, as they were called, took violent action. One was John Brown, a white man obsessed with the belief that armed revolt was necessary to free the slaves. Brown's zeal was remarkable. The distinguished black leader Frederick Douglass once noted that Brown was "as deeply interested in our cause, as though his own soul had been pierced with the iron of slavery."[7] Brown's dream of starting a race war to establish a state run by ex-slaves ended in 1859; while raiding a government arsenal, he was captured and hanged for treason.

In 1852 Dred Scott, a slave, took his master to court in an unsuccessful bid for his freedom.

Freeing the Slaves

By the time of Brown's raid, the always delicate political balance between free and slave-owning states had become a major issue. It deeply divided the country in the election that made Abraham Lincoln president in 1860. It was also a primary factor in the South's decision to secede, a move that led to the Civil War.

A crowd of blacks in Washington, D.C., celebrates the abolition of slavery in 1866. With the defeat of the Confederacy in the Civil War, Southern slaves were granted their freedom.

In 1862, while this conflict still raged, Lincoln announced that, as of January 1, 1863, all slaves in states or territories rebelling against the United States would no longer be in bondage. Although Lincoln's Emancipation Proclamation had little immediate effect, it was hailed by slaves, free blacks, and abolitionists as a great moral victory.

The bloody war finally ended in 1865 with the reunification of the country and the defeat of the Confederacy. The era that followed was called Reconstruction, since so much work was needed to rebuild the devastated South and to repair deep, lingering resentments on both sides. Reconstruction was a time of dramatic change for African Americans, especially the estimated 4 million newly freed slaves.

Although these ex-slaves were suddenly free, they were also poor. Nearly all were illiterate, and many were virtually homeless, having just been turned out of the only homes they had known. A major focus of Reconstruction, therefore, was an intense effort to improve their opportunities and living conditions. These efforts echoed words spoken by Frederick Douglass before the war: "We ask nothing at the hands of the American people but simple justice, and an equal chance to live."[8]

Legally Establishing Rights

Although now free, African Americans still lacked even basic rights such as legal protection. The Emancipation Proclamation had made no such provisions. Only individual state laws or a nationwide constitutional amendment could provide them.

During Reconstruction, three amendments to the Constitution were ratified. In 1865 the Thirteenth Amendment (echoing Lincoln's proclamation) formally abolished slavery. In 1868 the Fourteenth Amendment gave blacks full citizenship and equal protection under the law. In 1870 the Fifteenth Amendment prohibited states from denying any citizen the right to vote on the basis of race.

The government also passed a number of other laws that enforced or enhanced the constitutional amendments. For example, the Civil Rights Act of 1866 granted blacks a variety of rights, including the right to make contracts, sue and be sued, marry, travel, and own property. The Reconstruction Act of 1867, among other things, let them participate in the political arena by sitting in constitutional conventions or helping to draft state constitutions.

Jim Crow

These new laws were important, but they often had little effect on the day-to-day lives of African Americans. Furthermore, progress slowed dramatically when a conservative Republican, Rutherford B. Hayes, became president in 1877. His administration weakened federal civil rights policy and allowed several southern states to pass laws negating Reconstruction reforms.

These repressive statutes were called Jim Crow laws. (The name came from a caricature of a black man popularized by a white musician.) Specific Jim Crow laws varied by region, but all shared certain general characteristics. They typically kept blacks from voting through the use of unfair literacy tests or taxes. They restricted what jobs blacks could take and what neighborhoods they could live in. They prevented blacks from owning property or marrying outside their race. And they forced blacks to use separate public facilities.

Jim Crow also kept blacks from receiving adequate education. To white southerners, this was simply another way to keep blacks in their place. Hoke Smith, a governor of Georgia in the early twentieth century, commented, "Mere instruction from books will accomplish nothing for [the black man]. . . . The best educator he can have will be found in the white man who will control and direct him."[9]

Humiliation and Violence

Many other laws, less encompassing but still humiliating, were specific to certain states or cities. In South Carolina, for instance, blacks could not play checkers with whites in public. The races could not even look out the same factory window together. Sometimes Jim Crow was nothing more than unspoken, long-standing custom. Journalist Juan Williams notes,

Blacks were expected to tip their hats when they walked past whites, but whites did not have to remove their hats

Black children attend class at a segregated school in Virginia. Segregation statutes known as Jim Crow laws prevented Southern blacks from receiving an adequate education.

even when they entered a black family's home. Whites were to be called "sir" and "ma'am" by blacks, who in turn were called by their first names by whites. People with white skin were to be given a wide berth on the sidewalk; blacks were expected to step aside meekly.[10]

Violence against African Americans in the South—typically in the form of beatings, lynchings, and property destruction—was also common. In 1865 and 1866 alone some five thousand southern blacks were victims of racially motivated murders. Some attacks were by individuals, but organized groups were often behind them. The largest of these, the Ku Klux Klan, specialized in anonymous terror. Bands of white-robed, hooded Klansmen rode at night throughout rural America intimidating, beating, and sometimes killing those they opposed.

Plessy v. Ferguson

Although conditions for northern blacks were still inferior to those of whites, life for blacks in the North was better than in the South. Tolerance was greater, as were educational and work opportunities, and several states had individual laws barring racial discrimination. Civil rights organizations sprang up during this period. The most influential of these was the National Association for the Advancement of Colored People (NAACP), formed in 1909 by W.E.B. DuBois and others.

Such groups mounted a variety of legal contests. In 1891, for instance, a group of blacks in Louisiana challenged that state's Separate Car Law, which ordered railroads to provide equal but separate cars for blacks and whites. In this test case, a shoemaker named Homer A. Plessy was arrested after deliberately sitting in a whites-only coach. (Plessy, of mixed racial heritage, considered himself seven-eighths white and one-eighth black.)

In the ensuing trial, the state argued that its law was constitutional, as long as the services provided to each race were equal. Plessy's lawyers, however, maintained that the real question was whether the state could label citizens as white or black in the course of daily life. In 1896 the U.S. Supreme Court sided against Plessy, ruling that "separate but equal" public facilities were indeed constitutional.

Washington and DuBois

◼

During the late nineteenth and early twentieth centuries, Booker T. Washington and W.E.B. DuBois emerged as the primary leaders of the civil rights movement. They stood in sharp contrast: Washington favored integration into mainstream white society, while DuBois advocated a separation that would move blacks away from white-dominated society.

Washington believed that his race's best chance for advancement lay in industrial training that would improve individual independence and dignity. This was summarized in his 1895 "Atlanta Compromise" speech, which articulated his feeling that blacks and whites could remain separate if they worked together for mutual progress (quoted in Adam Fairclough's *Better Day Coming*): "In all things that are purely social we can be as separate as the fingers, yet as one hand in all things essential to mutual progress."

Meanwhile, DuBois—a Harvard-educated sociologist, writer, and leader—believed that only through political power and higher education could the black community compete on an equal footing with whites. In 1905 DuBois and other black leaders organized the Niagara movement. DuBois summarized its mission in a letter sent to potential backers and members (reprinted in Carson et al.'s *The Eyes on the Prize Civil Rights Reader.*) "The time seems more than ripe for an organized, determined, and aggressive action on the part of men who believe in Negro freedom and growth."

Booker T. Washington (left) and W.E.B. DuBois (right) were the primary leaders of the civil rights movement of the late nineteenth and early twentieth centuries.

This decision, known as *Plessy v. Ferguson*, was a serious blow to civil rights activists, because it formally justified Jim Crow laws. For the next fifty years, the South used the ruling to maintain segregation. History and religion professor Vincent Harding comments, "With that action, separate-but-equal became both the law of the land and the symbol of the fundamental schizophrenia at the heart of American democracy."[11]

Leaving the South

Plessy had a major impact on black Americans for decades. With no change in sight for their unequal job and educational opportunities, many African Americans had no recourse other than to accept low-paying jobs as farmhands, servants, or factory workers. More likely than not, they were constantly in debt to (white) landlords and merchants as well.

The oppression caused by Jim Crow laws led to a major demographic shift in the early part of the twentieth century. Between 1910 and 1930, an estimated 1 million blacks left the South in search of better jobs and lives. Many migrated to the rural West and Midwest; for example, by 1910 southern blacks had founded twenty-five all-black towns in Oklahoma. Hundreds of thousands moved to industrialized northern cities such as Chicago and Detroit.

There blacks found both new opportunities and new friction. Whites in the North, Midwest, and West found themselves competing with increasingly large numbers of blacks for the same jobs and housing. Occasionally, tension between the races erupted into violence.

For example, major race riots in Brownsville, Texas, in 1906 and in Springfield, Illinois, in 1908 left dozens dead and hundreds injured or homeless. During the "Red Summer" of 1919 (so named for the blood that flowed), twenty-five major race riots resulted in at least one hundred deaths and thousands of injuries. During this period, there were also hundreds of documented lynchings; no doubt, many more went unreported.

The Great War and the Depression

Along with migration patterns, another factor that affected the black community was World War I (1914–1918). Roughly

360,000 black Americans served in the U.S. armed forces, and for many it was their first exposure to life outside America. Perhaps they were not surprised to serve in all-black units that were poorly equipped and rarely placed in combat situations. However, many were shocked to see how little overt racism existed in France and other European nations. It struck these soldiers as cruelly ironic that they were denied democracy, justice, and freedom at home but were fighting for these same ideals overseas.

After the war, many returning veterans began advocating reforms that would provide more than rundown slums, the most menial jobs, or substandard schools for their children. As one black newspaper commented, "Negro soldiers returning from the war inflamed their people with stories of race equality in Europe."[12] However, significant change was hindered by the next major social development. In October 1929 the stock market crashed, sparking the devastating economic slump called the Great Depression.

Nearly all Americans faced extreme hardships then, but blacks were especially hard hit. Men desperate for work rode the rails from town to town; children sometimes ate garbage; and the homeless lived in shantytowns made of cardboard and scraps. Whites, equally desperate for work, were happy to take menial positions (such as maids, janitors, or busboys) traditionally held by blacks, and they were usually hired over blacks. As a result, unemployment in black communities often stood at 50 percent. The bitter joke was that blacks were "last hired and first fired."

World War II

America's involvement in World War II (1939–1945) ended the Great Depression and brought further changes for black Americans. Nearly 1 million African Americans joined the military. At first, their units were completely segregated. The legendary Tuskegee Airmen, for example, were America's first black military pilots. Furthermore, few blacks were assigned to combat duty, leading to persistent charges that military leaders assumed minorities were incapable of anything but the most menial labor.

As the war progressed, however, the armed forces became slowly and steadily integrated. In addition, the drastic need for defense-related factory workers at home prompted a new wave of

The Scottsboro Case

One of the most publicized civil rights cases in the years before the Second World War was the Scottsboro case. This was actually several court cases that lasted almost seven years, three of them tried before the U.S. Supreme Court.

The case began in 1931 in Scottsboro, Alabama, when a fight broke out among several teenagers, black and white, who were hitching rides on a train. The white passengers accused nine black men of raping two white women in the group. Eight of these so-called Scottsboro boys were sentenced to death. (The case of the ninth was declared a mistrial.) However, the Supreme Court overturned the convictions in 1932. It ruled that the defendants had not been well represented during their trials. Alabama officials refused to drop the case and began a series of new trials. By then, the case had attracted national attention.

The Alabama prosecutors secured two new convictions, but in 1935 the Supreme Court overturned these because no blacks had been allowed to serve on the juries. State officials once again refused to drop charges against any of the defendants. More trials in 1936 and 1937 resulted in long prison sentences for five of the defendants although charges against the remaining four were dropped. By 1950 four of the convicted men had served time and been paroled. The fifth escaped to Michigan, where the governor refused to surrender him to Alabama officials.

Young black men accused in the 1931 Scottsboro, Alabama, rape case are guarded by white police officers in this photo.

migration toward industrial jobs in the North and West. Black activists seized the opportunity created by these events to renew their calls for civil rights, especially on the home front. As the black newspaper *The Crisis* stated, "Now is the time *not* to be silent about the breaches in democracy in our own land."[13]

As a result, the civil rights battle continued in the nation's courtrooms, and during the early 1940s the NAACP was responsible for a number of major legal victories. For example, in 1940 the Supreme Court ruled in *Hansberry v. Lee* that it was unconstitutional to ban African Americans from white neighborhoods. Such decisions were small, incremental moves toward genuine equality.

The Next Level

In addition to courtroom battles, sporadic political protests had occurred even during the war. In 1941, for example, union leader A. Philip Randolph scored a major success. He threatened to organize a massive march in Washington, D.C., to protest defense-job discrimination. The protest was canceled when President Franklin D. Roosevelt, eager to defuse a potentially explosive incident, created a committee to investigate and prosecute workplace discrimination.

Two years later, in 1943, a new organization, the Congress of Racial Equality (CORE), held "sit-ins" at segregated restaurants in Chicago, Detroit, Denver, and other cities. In these peaceful protests, protesters deliberately courted arrest to test the constitutionality of segregation. They took seats (or sat on the floor) in sections reserved for whites only, sometimes waiting all day while the restaurant staff refused to serve them.

Gradually, a concerted, organized civil rights movement was emerging. Activist organizations such as CORE and the NAACP were attracting record numbers of members and drawing increased financial support from whites and blacks alike. Furthermore, a new generation of activists was coming of age, in particular a group of bright young lawyers who would take the fight to the next level.

Chapter Two

Postwar Progress

The next developments in the civil rights movement were, in some ways, inspired by the Allied victory in World War II. At great cost Americans and their allies had defeated Nazism and fascism, serious threats to human rights. Also, the United Nations was born in the aftermath of the war, and its strong commitment to worldwide human rights further inspired civil rights activists. For the first time in history, the United States was nurturing a generation of young black Americans with a global point of view.

These emerging activists joined their predecessors in helping to bring about a number of landmark advances in civil rights during the immediate postwar years. For example, they called for Harry Truman (who had succeeded Roosevelt as president in 1945) to order the complete integration of the armed forces. They also succeeded in creating a federal program to help minorities obtain government jobs. Furthermore, they made sure that black veterans (like their white counterparts) would be eligible for free college education through a benefits program called the G.I. Bill.

Separate but Unequal

The NAACP, as the nation's foremost civil rights group, was at the forefront of this process, its focus the reform of existing laws. Its first goal was to overturn the Supreme Court's ruling on *Plessy v. Ferguson*. This was the ruling that for decades had been used to justify racial discrimination with "separate but equal" facilities that were indeed separate but were rarely, if ever, equal.

The stark difference in supposedly equal facilities was nowhere more apparent than in education. Throughout the South, schools for white students were well supported, well staffed, and well supplied. Schools for black students, meanwhile, were poorly equipped and poorly funded.

Buildings for black students frequently suffered from leaky roofs, crumbling walls, pest infestations, or poor heating. As late as 1950, many black schools in South Carolina had no buses, lunchrooms, gyms, or even indoor toilets. Teachers in these schools were underpaid, overworked, and often poorly trained. Furthermore, although a handful of distinguished African American colleges existed, black students had few opportunities to seek anything beyond the most basic education. In 1939 journalist Gould Beech noted the overall disparity:

> For each dollar spent on the education of the average child in the nation, the South spends 50 cents for each of its white children, 14 cents for each of its Negro children. While the region as a whole spends approximately one fourth the amount for each Negro child that it does for each white child, there is a considerable variation from state to

Despite "separate but equal" laws in place since the *Plessy v. Ferguson* ruling of 1892, schools for black students (left) were largely inferior to those for white students (right).

state. The ratio is more than 1-to-9 in Mississippi, 1-to-8 in South Carolina.[14]

Sweatt v. Painter

The NAACP's attack on *Plessy* concentrated on cases involving education, in part because the disparities of the "separate but equal" concept in schooling were so stark. Specifically, it argued that civil rights of equal protection under the law—as stipulated in the Fourteenth Amendment—were being denied to black students because they were being segregated.

An important early milestone was a case called *Sweatt v. Painter*. It was named for Heman Marion Sweatt, a black student who had applied to the University of Texas Law School in 1946. The school had denied Sweatt admission solely because of his race. It offered him instead a place in a law school designed just for black students. (No such school had existed before; the state hastily created it in the wake of Sweatt's first appeals.)

Sweatt declined the state's offer, arguing that he could not receive an equal education in the blacks-only school because the newer school was inadequate. For example, the University of Texas Law School had sixteen full-time and three part-time professors; the school for blacks had only five full-time professors. The whites-only school had 850 students and a law library of 65,000 volumes; the black school had 23 students and a library of 16,500 volumes. Furthermore, the blacks-only school was not fully accredited. Sweatt argued that, because of this lack of accreditation, his chances of getting a good job after graduation would be significantly lower.

Victory

A gifted young attorney named Thurgood Marshall led the NAACP's legal team when it argued Sweatt's case before the U.S. Supreme Court. Marshall made it clear that his intent was to force a ruling with broader implications than "separate but equal." He declared, "The attack is upon segregation and nothing else. I want this court to know that I don't care how equal those schools are, if they were exact duplicates, with the same faculty and to the ounce in cement. They are segregated and cannot be equal in any sense of the word."[15]

The Court agreed with Marshall's argument, ruling unanimously in Sweatt's favor in 1950. It found the segregation at the

University of Texas Law School to be unconstitutional and therefore illegal, and it ordered the school to be integrated. Chief Justice Frederick M. Vinson wrote, "The legal education offered [Sweatt] is not substantially equal to that which he would receive if admitted to the University of Texas Law School; and the Equal Protection Clause of the Fourteenth Amendment requires that he be admitted to the University of Texas Law School."[16]

Civil rights activists across the country hailed the decision as a major step forward. The comments of W.A. Folkes, the managing editor of the *Atlanta Daily World* newspaper, were typical. He stated that the decision "certainly will be a means by which the South will join in the parade of democracy."[17]

However, the decision was condemned just as roundly by segregationists. Georgia governor Herman Talmadge, for instance, declared: "As long as I am governor, Negroes will not be admitted to white schools. The line is drawn. The threats that have been held over the head of the South for four years are now pointed like a dagger ready to be plunged into the very heart of southern tradition."[18]

McLaurin v. Oklahoma

That same year, the Court ruled on a related case called *McLaurin v. Oklahoma*. The case began when the University of Oklahoma was forced to admit G.W. McLaurin, a black retired professor who wanted to earn a doctorate in education. Oklahoma's university system did not offer postgraduate programs for black students, but, after McLaurin sued, it did admit him to its otherwise all-white graduate school.

School authorities forced McLaurin to sit in isolation, far away from other students in classrooms. He was also forced to sit away from other students when studying in the library or eating in the cafeteria. For a period of time, McLaurin's seats were surrounded by rails on which were hung signs stating, "Reserved for Colored."

McLaurin argued that this isolation was unfair, in part because he was denied the usual give-and-take with other students that is an important part of graduate study. Journalist Juan Williams notes, "Although he attended the same classes, ate the same food, and studied from the same books as the other students, he was not getting an equal education because of the daily harassments and restrictions."[19]

The NAACP legal team argued many cases before the U.S. Supreme Court, including the *McLaurin v. Oklahoma* case of 1950 that challenged segregation in institutes of higher learning.

Setting the Stage

As had *Sweatt*, *McLaurin* reached the Supreme Court, where the NAACP legal team argued that McLaurin's rights of equal protection were being violated. Once again, the Court unanimously agreed. It ruled in 1950 that a public institution of higher learning could not provide different treatment to a student solely because of race.

Specifically, the Court said, this was because forced isolation violated McLaurin's rights and hampered his education. Writing on behalf of the Court, Chief Justice Vinson noted, "The restrictions imposed upon [McLaurin] impair and inhibit his ability to study, to engage in discussions and exchange views with other students, and, in general, to learn his profession."[20]

The Court's rulings in both *Sweatt* and *McLaurin* set crucial precedents for decisions in later court cases, notably *Brown v. Board of Education of Topeka, Kansas*. This 1954 case was one of the most far-reaching Supreme Court decisions in the twentieth century, and arguably one of the most important legal decisions in American history.

Brown v. Board of Education

Brown began as a challenge to a Kansas statute that permitted cities with populations of more than fifteen thousand to maintain segregated public schools. The Topeka school system had used this statute to establish separate elementary schools. (Other public schools in the city were not segregated.)

A black railroad worker named Oliver Brown objected to this policy. His daughter Linda, unable to attend an all-white school a few blocks from their house, had to walk through a hazardous railroad switchyard to a bus stop, then ride a mile to an all-black school. Williams notes, "It wasn't the worst that black children had to endure, but soft-spoken Oliver Brown was fed up with his child having to go to the other side of town when there was a good school much closer to home—a white school."[21]

Brown, arguing that this situation violated Linda's Fourteenth Amendment rights, sued the school board. As the case worked its

The *McLaurin* Decision

◼

One of the important Supreme Court decisions leading to the landmark *Brown* case was *McLaurin v. Oklahoma.* In giving voice to the Court's decision, Chief Justice Frederick M. Vinson made the following comments, which are excerpted in *McLaurin v. Oklahoma State Regents* on the Afro-American History Website.

Our society grows increasingly complex, and our need for trained leaders increases correspondingly. Appellant's [McLaurin's] case represents, perhaps, the epitome of that need, for he is attempting to obtain an advanced degree in education, to become, by definition, a leader and trainer of others. Those who will come under his guidance and influence must be directly affected by the education he receives. Their own education and development will necessarily suffer to the extent that his training is unequal to that of his classmates. State-imposed restrictions which produce such inequalities cannot be sustained.

way through the courts, the board of education defended its position. It argued, among other things, that segregated schools were good because they prepared black children for the segregation they would surely face during adulthood. It also argued that segregated schools were not necessarily harmful, since distinguished black Americans such as Frederick Douglass and Booker T. Washington had attended segregated schools and still achieved great things.

A federal district court hearing the case acknowledged Brown's position. As one of the judges noted in his opinion, "Segregation of white and colored children in public schools has a detrimental effect upon the colored children. . . . A sense of inferiority affects the motivation of a child to learn."[22]

Arguing the Case

Despite its sympathetic outlook, however, the district court found no precedent allowing it to overturn *Plessy*. It claimed that the schools in question were sufficiently equal in buildings, transportation, teaching standards, and teachers. The court therefore denied that Linda Brown's rights were being violated.

Meanwhile, several other similar cases were working their way through the courts. Buoyed by its victories in *Sweatt* and *McLaurin*, the NAACP decided to combine the Brown case with cases from South Carolina, Virginia, and Delaware when it argued the issue before the Supreme Court. Collectively, these cases were called *Brown v. Board of Education.*

Thurgood Marshall, again representing the NAACP, argued once more that racial segregation in public schools clearly harmed minority students and interfered with their ability to learn. This separation, he stated, hurt the "development of the personalities of [black] children" because it "deprived them of equal status in the school community . . . destroying their self-respect."[23]

Striking Down "Separate but Equal"

The nation was closely attuned to how the Court would decide this important case. When the ruling was issued on May 17, 1954, it was a clear victory for civil rights advocates. The Court unanimously agreed that separate educational facilities were inherently unequal and therefore unconstitutional. Chief Justice

Earl Warren noted, "Does segregation of children in public schools solely on the basis of race, even though the physical facilities and other 'tangible' factors may be equal, deprive the children of the minority group of equal educational opportunities? We believe that it does."[24]

The *Brown* decision was somewhat limited. It affected only public schools; the issue of segregation in other public areas, such as restaurants or restrooms, was not addressed. Also, the decision did not require public schools to desegregate by a specific time, only "with all deliberate speed." Some advocates of integration were disappointed with this vague wording. They knew that implementing the decision would be a tough, protracted battle. As Marshall noted, "We will have to go from state to state and county to county."[25]

Nonetheless, *Brown* was clearly an important victory for civil rights, and its supporters hailed it as a turning point. An editorial in the *Washington Post* noted, "It is not too much to speak of the Court's decision as a new birth of freedom. . . . Abroad as well as at home, this decision will engender a renewal of faith in democratic institutions and ideals."[26]

Thurgood Marshall (right) meets with the opposing attorney, John Davis, in the 1954 *Brown v. Board of Education* case. The ruling in the case was a huge victory for civil rights advocates.

"The End of Civilization" and Renewed Violence

At the opposite end of the political spectrum, the response was swift to "Black Monday," as the decision became known among segregationists. South Carolina's governor, James F. Byrnes, spoke for these opponents when he stated, "Ending segregation would mark the beginning of the end of civilization as we have known it."[27] An editorial in the Jackson, Mississippi, *Daily News* added, "Human blood may stain southern soil in many places because of this decision, but the dark red stains of that blood will be on the marble of the United States Supreme Court Building."[28]

Resentment among segregationists over the *Brown* decision was probably at least partly responsible for a renewed wave of violence across the South. The most sensational incident was the killing of Emmett Till, a fourteen-year-old from Chicago, in the summer of 1955. While visiting relatives in Money, Mississippi, Till spoke (on a dare) to a white woman in a grocery store. (Some accounts say he whistled at her as well.) For this offense, Till was tortured, shot, and drowned. Two white men, including the woman's husband, were accused of the crime, but in a highly publicized trial they were acquitted.

Till's murder shocked the nation in a way no abstract legal argument could—especially after newspapers across the country published graphic photos of Till's funeral. The boy's mother had insisted on an open casket; she wanted to dramatically demonstrate what her son had suffered. Preachers across the country gave impassioned sermons based on the murder, and contributions to organizations like the NAACP poured in because of the publicity. Juan Williams comments, "It is difficult to measure just how profound an effect the public viewing of Till's body created. But without question it moved black America in a way the Supreme Court ruling on school desegregation could not match."[29]

Jackie Robinson

The courtroom was not the only venue for civil rights advocacy during this period. The cultural arena—the world of sports, music, and the arts—was also undergoing change. For example, black actors had long been overlooked in Hollywood, relegated to small or demeaning roles. This began to change in 1940, when

Baseball commissioner Ford Frick presents Jackie Robinson with an award in 1950. Robinson, the first black major league player, was a star with the Brooklyn Dodgers.

Hattie McDaniel became the first African American to win an Academy Award. The honor came with a slap in the face, however: McDaniel won the Oscar (for her supporting role in *Gone with the Wind*), but she and the film's other black actors had not even been invited to its premiere party.

Another dramatic breakthrough of the color barrier in this period came in the field of sports. It is almost inconceivable today, but for sixty years there were no black players in Major League Baseball. The situation changed forever when a brilliant athlete named Jackie Robinson stepped onto Ebbets Field as a Brooklyn Dodger in April 1947.

Robinson, the first black major league baseball player since 1887, endured hate letters, insults, fastballs aimed at his head and legs, catchers spitting on his shoes, and even death threats. On the other hand, Robinson had many supporters, inside and outside pro ball. When some members of the St. Louis Cardinals called for a strike against the Dodgers, Major League Baseball commissioner Ford Frick replied, "I don't care if half the league strikes. This is the United States of America, and one citizen has as much right to play as another."[30]

Robinson endured with grace, dignity, and strength. He quickly became the Dodgers' top star, as well as a symbol of hope for millions of black Americans and a hero for future generations.

Singing at Constitution Hall

In 1939 the distinguished opera singer Marian Anderson tried to book a recital at Constitution Hall, one of Washington, D.C.'s most prestigious halls. However, the Daughters of the American Revolution (DAR), which managed the hall, barred her performance as a "singer of color." This decision caused a storm of protest, including First Lady Eleanor Roosevelt's resignation from the DAR. Roosevelt then helped organize an open-air recital for Anderson at the Lincoln Memorial, which drew a crowd of seventy-five thousand and was broadcast by radio to millions.

Anderson continued to break barriers. She was the first black artist to sing a leading role at New York City's Metropolitan Opera. Finally, in 1953, she had another chance to perform at Constitution Hall, before a packed and adoring crowd.

Marian Anderson performs at the Lincoln Memorial in 1939 after she was barred from Washington D.C.'s Constitution Hall.

Another baseball icon, Hank Aaron, once remarked, "They say certain people are bigger than life, but Jackie Robinson is the only man I've known who truly was."[31]

As pioneers such as McDaniel and Robinson made their contributions to the nation's culture, others were striving for different victories. Full equality remained a far-off dream, and resistance to integration, especially in the South, remained strong. A concerted effort was needed to further the cause. It would come in the arenas of public transportation and education.

Chapter Three

Victories in Montgomery and Little Rock

In the mid-1950s, civil rights activists focused on the fields of school and transportation desegregation. These tested the strength of the *Brown* decision, pushed its limits, and forced reluctant authorities to observe the law. To dramatize their concerns and alert the public, activists organized several major protests.

One of the most important of these was in 1955–1956 in Montgomery, Alabama, when the city's black population refused to use its segregated bus system, a system that depended on a largely black ridership for its profitability. This protest was a stunning success for the civil rights movement. It forced the city to desegregate the buses. Its dramatic events also became headline news nationwide, gripping America and alerting millions outside the South to the urgent situation. To many observers, the Montgomery bus boycott was the true beginning of the civil rights era.

"The Only Tired I Was, Was Tired of Giving In"

Like all southern cities, Montgomery had laws designed to maintain segregation. From drinking fountains to restaurant seating to public benches, city facilities were limited to use by whites or blacks.

The bus system was just one more way in which custom and law kept Montgomery's black residents separate and humiliated.

Black bus riders in Montgomery paid their fares at the front, but (unlike whites) they then had to exit and reboard at the rear. Once aboard, they were confined to rows behind a movable barrier. As the bus filled, this barrier was pushed back to create priority room for whites.

On December 1, 1955, Rosa Parks, a forty-two-year-old black seamstress, took a bus to get home from her job at the Montgomery Fair department store. She and three other blacks sat in the first row of the "colored section." A few stops after Parks boarded, the white section filled and one white man was still standing.

The driver asked passengers in Parks's row to move back. Three complied; she did not. Contrary to legend, Parks did not refuse simply because she was exhausted from work. As she later wrote, "No, the only tired I was, was tired of giving in."[32]

The Boycott Begins

When Parks was arrested and jailed for her offense, word spread quickly through Montgomery's black community. An NAACP official, E.D. Nixon, arranged bail for her. He then asked Parks to allow the incident to be the linchpin of a formal protest.

Activists had long considered boycotting the Montgomery buses. However, they had been waiting until a well-respected community member took action. Parks was not the first black person to refuse to give up a bus seat (or even the first in Montgomery), but she was the right one: dignified and educated, a longtime NAACP member, and with a spotless reputation.

Parks consented, even though her husband worried that "the white folks will kill you, Rosa."[33] Nixon and his colleagues then organized a one-day boycott. They asked people to shun buses on the day of Parks's trial, the Monday after her Thursday arrest.

Over the weekend, word spread. Jo Ann Robinson of the Women's Political Council oversaw the writing and distribution of thirty-five thousand handbills. The ministers in the organizing group also announced the event in their Sunday sermons. Among the clergy were Ralph Abernathy of the First Baptist Church; Robert Graetz, a white Lutheran minister; and a recent arrival in

A police officer fingerprints Rosa Parks in December 1955. Parks's arrest for refusing to give up her seat on a city bus to a white man sparked the Montgomery bus boycott.

Montgomery, Dr. Martin Luther King Jr., the new pastor of the Dexter Avenue Baptist Church.

A Leader

The organizers estimated that the protest would be successful if 60 percent of the city's black bus riders cooperated. They were stunned on Monday morning to see that virtually everyone heeded the call. African Americans who usually took the bus to work—roughly three-quarters of the regular patrons—took taxis, walked, or caught rides instead. Some even rode mules. Historian Taylor Branch writes, "In spite of the bitter morning cold, their fear of white people and their desperate need for wages, Montgomery Negroes were turning the City Bus Lines into a ghost fleet."[34]

Parks was convicted that day. (She was fined $10, plus $4 in court fees.) Nonetheless, Montgomery's activists were jubilant when they met that evening and voted overwhelmingly to continue the boycott. Organizing themselves as the Montgomery Improvement Association (MIA), they elected King as their president.

Martin Luther King Jr. was an eloquent and inspirational speaker. Here, he delivers a speech about the importance of nonviolence to supporters in a Montgomery church.

King, only twenty-six years old, was chosen for several reasons. He was well educated (he had a doctorate in theology from Boston University) and, as a minister, respected as a spiritual leader. He was also new in town, and therefore viewed as impartial by the diverse and sometimes fractious elements within Montgomery's black community. Furthermore, King was an articulate and inspirational speaker. To an overflow meeting of boycott supporters at a church that night, he delivered a speech that eloquently expressed the community's hopes:

We are here this evening for serious business. We are here in a general sense because first and foremost, we are American citizens, and we are determined to acquire our citizenship to the fullness of its meaning. We are here also because of our deep-seated belief that democracy transformed from thin paper to thick action is the greatest form of government on earth.[35]

Extending the Boycott

The MIA hoped that a compromise would be quickly reached. Four days in, it offered authorities a modest plan, asking for little more than assurances of polite treatment by drivers, an end to segregated buses, and the hiring of black bus drivers for the city's "Negro routes." Authorities refused to consider the compromise. Commissioner Clyde Sellers stated, "If we granted the Negroes these demands, they would go about boasting of a victory that they had won over the white people, and this we will not stand for."[36]

Stung, the MIA voted to continue the boycott indefinitely. When days and weeks passed and the buses remained empty, authorities tried to forcibly end the protest. They first cracked down on black cab services, which had started charging 10 cents a ride, the same as the bus fare. Officials threatened to arrest any cab driver charging less than the standard rate, which, with its 45-cent minimum, was beyond the daily budgets of most blacks.

The MIA countered with a complex but effective "private taxi" system. Cars in this system (including "rolling churches" bought for the purpose by religious groups) carpooled passengers to and from central points. In addition, some of Montgomery's white housewives, unwilling to do without maids, nannies, and gardeners, gave rides to their employees.

The city commission then falsely announced that the boycott was over, hoping to fool people into riding again. The MIA learned of the hoax on a Saturday; the story was due to run in Sunday's paper. MIA officials foiled the plot by going bar-hopping Saturday night to spread the word.

Conspiracy Charges

As weeks turned into months, authorities tried other ways to break the boycott. For example, owners of the private taxis found their liability insurance repeatedly canceled. Passengers waiting for carpools were arrested for loitering, and drivers were arrested for such minor infractions as overloading their cars. The situation occasionally turned violent as well: The homes of several activists (including King) were bombed, fortunately without serious injury.

Authorities also tried to stop the boycott through legal maneuvers. Eighty-nine protest leaders were indicted on charges of conspiracy. It became a point of honor to present oneself at

A White Southerner's Reaction to the Boycott

This open letter to the black population of Montgomery, Alabama, was published in the *Montgomery Advertiser* on January 13, 1956, about a month after the beginning of the bus boycott there. It is reprinted in "White and Opposition Reaction," on the Montgomery Bus Boycott Homepage.

Editor, The Advertiser:

The white people of Montgomery are typical of the other white people of America, slow to anger and slow to make up their minds. But once they do they have always come out victorious.

The bus fare has already been raised 50%. Should you continue the bus boycott six months the loss would be repaid in 18 months and you will keep on paying and paying as long as you live. So what have you gained?

Where is your appreciation, your sense of duty? Look around your home. Who furnished "know how" to prepare your foods and medicines, give you electricity, make your clothes, design and build your cars and every other convenience that you so richly enjoy, that goes with civilization. Now what have you done for yourself?

You are indebted to the white people of Montgomery for life itself. As the white doctor brought most of you into the world. The white man paid about 95 percent for your education, furnished you jobs and a place to live, etc. Now suppose the white people of Montgomery would not hire you any longer or give you a place to live, where would you go or [what would you] do?

(signed) Hill Lindsay

the courthouse for arrest on these charges. Lutheran minister Robert Graetz recalled, "The most disappointed people in Montgomery were Negro leaders who were not indicted."[37]

In March, King was the first of these protesters to be tried. He was convicted and fined $500, plus $500 in court costs. The high-profile trial helped the MIA attract national attention for its cause. It also did much to foster King's rise to national fame. The minister appeared on the covers of *Time* and the *New York Times Magazine* soon after his conviction.

The Boycott Ends

As the boycott dragged on through the summer, Montgomery's business community grew increasingly frustrated. The city's business owners were generally opposed to integration, but the boycott was bad for them. Without transportation, Montgomery's fifty thousand black residents rarely shopped downtown, and revenues were dropping.

The MIA also hoped the boycott would end. However, it wanted it to end only on its terms and without compromise. Acting on the MIA's behalf, the NAACP therefore took the case to the Supreme Court, arguing that the *Brown* decision should apply to other public facilities besides schools. In November 1956 the Court agreed, declaring that segregation on public buses was unconstitutional.

The euphoric MIA called an end to the boycott, cautioning people to avoid the buses until the official government ruling arrived on December 20. On that day, an integrated group of protest leaders triumphantly rode the buses, sitting wherever they chose. The next day the black citizens of Montgomery did the same. They had endured more than a year of carpooling and walking—plus daily harassment, fear, and occasional violence—to achieve their goal.

The Aftermath

In the wake of the bus boycott, a major new civil rights organization emerged. The Southern Christian Leadership Conference (SCLC) was formed in Atlanta, Georgia, in 1957, with Martin Luther King as its first president. Composed primarily of religious leaders from across the South, it was designed to coordinate civil rights protests nationally.

Meanwhile, white backlash against the movement simmered across the South. More than one hundred members of Congress signed a document condemning *Brown* as an abuse of judicial power and declaring that the ruling would destroy the "amicable relations" between whites and blacks. Associations such as the

White Citizens Council were also organized in various cities to intimidate and undermine civil rights supporters. A particular emphasis was put on shutting down the NAACP in southern states.

Little Rock

The backlash grew stronger and came to a head in 1957 over the issue of school desegregation. Its focus became Central High School in Little Rock, Arkansas. Activists had chosen this school as a testing ground for enforcing the *Brown* ruling.

Little Rock, the state capital, was in some ways an unlikely location for a civil rights battle. Compared with other southern cities, its public facilities were relatively integrated. For example, the medical school at the public university there had been admitting black students since the late 1940s, and by 1957 nearly half of the university's graduate students were black. Little Rock had a few black policemen as well, and its libraries, parks, and public buses were integrated.

The city's school board thus had some reason to believe that it could desegregate peacefully. Only five days after the *Brown* ruling, the board had stated its intent to comply. Its desegregation plan included choosing nine volunteers to be the first black students at all-white Central High. As the beginning of the school year neared, many local activists were hopeful; in the words of one, Daisy Bates, "the time for delay, evasion, or procrastination was over."[38]

The nine chosen students were also full of hope, with little idea of the storm that was about to erupt around them. One student, Melba Patillo Beals, remarked, "There was no thought on my part, on anyone's part, that our going to Central High would trigger this terrible catastrophe. I wanted to go because [students at Central] had more privileges. They had more equipment; they had five floors of opportunity."[39]

Bringing In Troops

Little Rock's segregationists tried hard to stop the process. Among the reasons cited was the potential for violence. The reaction of Mrs. Clyde A. Thomason, a member of the Mothers' League of Little Rock Central High School, was typical. She testified at a meeting that she "had been told that the mothers were terrified to send their children to Central because of a rumor that the white and Negro youths were forming gangs and some of them were armed with guns and knives."[40]

On September 2, Arkansas governor Orval Faubus tried to stop the process. He ordered the state's National Guard to surround Central High and block the nine from entering. In a televised speech that night, Faubus stated that "blood would run in the streets"[41] if the students were allowed into Central. Bates commented later about this inflammatory speech: "In a half-dozen ill-chosen words, Faubus made his contribution to the mass hysteria that was to grip the city of Little Rock for several months."[42]

September 4 was the day the Little Rock Nine, as they became known, were scheduled to begin classes. Eight of them gathered near the school to walk in together, but the National Guard blocked them. The ninth, Elizabeth Eckford, never received the message to meet the others and tried to enter the school alone. An angry mob confronted her as guardsmen looked on. Before serious violence erupted, two white citizens stepped forward to help the terrified Elizabeth escape onto a bus and return home.

Trying to Attend School

On September 20, the NAACP got an injunction preventing Faubus from using the National Guard to block the school. The troops were withdrawn, but on September 23, the next school day, a mob of about one thousand gathered in front of Central High. While waiting for the students to arrive, the crowd beat up several black reporters from northern papers.

The mob erupted when word spread that the black students, escorted by local police, had entered the school through a side door. An Associated Press reporter described the scene: "'They've gone in,' a man roared. 'Oh, God, the niggers are in the school.' . . . 'Oh, my God,' [a] woman screamed. She burst into tears and tore at her hair. Hysteria swept the crowd."[43]

Fearful that police could not control the crowd, school administrators decided to send the black students home before noon. Eventually, the mob in front of the school dispersed, but the situation remained tense. Asked to describe the city's mood that night, the editor of the *Arkansas Gazette* stated, "I'll give it to you in one sentence. The police have been routed, the mob is in the streets and we're close to a reign of terror."[44]

Federal troops escort black students to school after the 1957 integration of Central High School in Little Rock, Arkansas.

Going to School with Soldiers

Two Arkansas politicians, U.S. congressman Brooks Hays and Little Rock mayor Woodrow Mann, asked President Dwight D. Eisenhower to intervene. The president, no great supporter of integration, was reluctant to anger influential southern politicians but wanted to avoid violent confrontation. Eisenhower also hoped to avoid inflaming a situation that put America in a bad light abroad. He stated,

> It would be difficult to exaggerate the harm that is being done to the prestige and influence and indeed to the safety of our nation and the world. Our enemies are gloating over this incident and using it everywhere to misrepresent our whole nation.[45]

Eisenhower eventually did take action. He sent one thousand paratroopers from the 101st Airborne Division of the U.S. Army into Little Rock. He also federalized the Arkansas National Guard, thus removing Faubus's control over it.

After that, on each school day troops escorted the Little Rock Nine to and from Central High in an armed convoy, patrolling outside during classes. In addition, each black student was assigned a personal military guard during school hours. Beals recalled, "The troops were wonderful. They were disciplined, they were attentive, they were caring, they didn't baby us, but they were there."[46]

"One Down . . . Eight to Go"

The majority of students at Central remained relatively polite, at least during school hours. Only a handful, mostly troublemakers known then as "juvenile delinquents," overtly tormented the Nine. Historian Taylor Branch notes, "Nearly all of them opposed integration, but those who [actively harassed] generally came from the same minority of troublemakers who refused to tuck in their shirts."[47]

Although this group was small, it nonetheless made life miserable for the Nine. The troublemakers shouted insults, vandalized lockers, threw flaming paper wads, and threatened to spray acid on the black students. The Nine mostly withstood the abuse, but their endurance had limits. In December, for instance, Minnijean Brown lost her temper. Another black student, Ernest Green, recalled the incident:

> Minni was about five-foot-ten, and this fellow couldn't have been more than five-five, five-four. [H]e reminded me of a small dog, yelping at somebody's leg. Minni had just picked up her chili, and before I could even say "Minni, why don't you tell him to shut up?" Minni had . . . dumped it on this dude's head. There was absolute silence in the place, and then the [cafeteria] help, all black, broke into applause.[48]

Minnijean was only suspended briefly for this incident. Later in the year, however, she was expelled after a shouting match with another girl. After her expulsion, some of the white students printed and passed around cards that read "One down . . . eight to go."

Closing Schools

There were other incidents—the school principal's life was threatened, and there were bomb threats—but gradually the harassment faded. The army troops left at the end of November, though the National Guardsmen remained for the rest of the school year.

The Little Rock Nine, minus Minnijean Brown, attended commencement that spring. Senior Ernest Green, the lone minority student in a class of 602, became Central High's first black graduate. Ernest recalled the ceremony, which was attended by reporters from all over the country: "I knew that once I got as far as that principal and received that diploma, I had cracked the wall."[49]

Meanwhile, Governor Faubus remained defiant. The state legislature passed a bill granting him the power to shut down Arkansas's public schools, and when the school year ended he closed all four of Little Rock's high schools. Faubus insisted this was not his fault: "If Daisy Bates would find an honest job and go to work, and if the U.S. Supreme Court would keep its cotton-picking hands off the Little Rock School Board's affairs, we could open the Little Rock schools!"[50]

A Movement Is Born

Other states followed Faubus's lead. Between 1957 and 1959, authorities in Virginia, Georgia, and Alabama closed some of their public schools to avoid integration. In 1959, however, these laws were declared unconstitutional and the schools, now integrated, reopened.

By this time, images of events in Little Rock and Montgomery —ranging from vicious mobs to stoic resistance—had saturated television news programs and newspaper reports around the

Ernest Green (fourth row, center) became the first African American to graduate from Arkansas's Central High School in 1958.

"That's the Way I Saw It"

James Meredith, the first black person to attend "Ole Miss," the University of Mississippi, in Oxford, could do so only with the protection of federal troops. He wrote an essay shortly after his admittance, which was published in the *Saturday Evening Post* on November 10, 1962, and is excerpted in Nick Treanor's *The Civil Rights Movement*.

> Through all that has happened I have tried to remain detached and objective. . . . When I was in the middle of the force of marshals being gathered to take me to Oxford I thought, personally, how utterly ridiculous this was, what a terrible waste of time and money and energy, to iron out some rough spots in our civilization. But realistically I knew that these changes were necessary. . . .
>
> When we were turned away the first time I tried to register at the university, and especially the second time, at the State Capitol in Jackson, I saw the mobs and heard them jeering, "Go home, nigger" and that stuff, but I never recognized them as individuals at all, even those who showed the greatest contempt for me. I felt they were not personally attacking me but that they were protesting a change and this was something they felt they must do. I thought it was impersonal. Some of them were crying, and their crying indicated to me even more the pain of change and the fear of things they did not know. . . . The people were bound to act that way, and it didn't really have anything to do with me personally. That's the way I saw it.

country. Black leaders and sympathetic whites across America responded, and a massive movement that was national in scope but focused on the South was under way. Montgomery and Little Rock had demonstrated how far black Americans would go to seek their rights; they also showed how far some southerners would go to prevent them. The stage was set for even more dramatic incidents.

Chapter Four

Sit-Ins and Freedom Rides

By the start of the 1960s, in the wake of events in Montgomery and Little Rock, the federal government was slowly enacting serious civil rights laws. But the government was moving too cautiously for many activists. They wanted to step up the pace of change. Forcing the issue meant, among other things, finding new fields of battle.

One of the most obvious was the restaurant business. In the South, restaurants were segregated, and the better ones were off-limits to blacks. (Some northern restaurants were also segregated.) To call attention to this inequity, activists organized protests called sit-ins. As the name suggests, these demonstrations consisted of people simply sitting down and refusing to leave until they got what they wanted.

Greensboro

Sit-ins were not a new tactic. On a limited scale, the first such demonstrations in America had taken place in the early 1940s, when CORE conducted sit-ins at segregated restaurants in Chicago and other northern cities. At least fifteen other civil rights sit-ins were reported in the United States during the 1950s.

These actions had generated little in publicity or results. However, by 1960 the civil rights movement was becoming big news everywhere. As a result, a sit-in that began as a small protest in a Woolworth store in Greensboro, North Carolina, created world-wide interest and sparked a massive wave of protest.

The Woolworth chain—a dime store and lunch-counter fixture in nearly every American downtown—was fully integrated outside the South. Its southern stores, however, had a double standard. Black patrons could shop for general merchandise or eat at stand-up snack bars, but they could not sit at Woolworth's popular lunch counters.

Acting on their own, four black freshmen at North Carolina Agricultural and Technical College decided to challenge the hypocrisy of having one section of the store off-limits. On February 1, 1960, Joseph McNeil, Franklin McCain, David Richmond, and Ezell Blair Jr. entered the Greensboro Woolworth. Each bought a few items in various departments. Then they sat down at the lunch counter and ordered food.

The Protest Builds

This was a bold move. At first, the counter's white patrons were silent and the white waitresses ignored the students. (Typically, most of the kitchen workers, and a few waitresses, were black.) One black waitress scolded them: "Fellows like you make our race look bad."[51]

Undaunted, the students silently remained in place, even though they knew the probability of being arrested—or worse—was high. The store manager called a policeman, but the officer could not do anything as long as the protest was not disruptive. Franklin McCain later recalled the policeman's anger:

You had the feeling that this is the first time that this big bad man with the gun and the club has been pushed in a corner. . . . We've provoked him, yes, but we haven't provoked him outwardly enough for him to resort to violence. And I think this is just killing him; you can see it all over him.[52]

The four men stayed until the store closed, then returned to their school's campus and began recruiting others. New protesters, including some whites, joined them in the next days, the numbers increasing as word spread and the news media picked

From Fear to Elation

The four college students who started the Greensboro sit-in acted on the spur of the moment, without a clear plan of action or a large organization behind them. Historian Taylor Branch explains their unlikely success in *Parting the Waters*.

No one had time to wonder why the Greensboro sit-in was so different. In the previous three years, similar demonstrations had occurred in at least sixteen other cities. Few of them made the news, all faded quickly from public notice, and none had the slightest catalytic effect anywhere else. By contrast, Greensboro helped define the new decade. Almost certainly, the lack of planning helped create the initial euphoria. Because the four students at Woolworth's had no plan, they began with no self-imposed limitations. They defined no tactical goals. They did not train or drill in preparation. They did not dwell on the many forces that might be used against them. Above all, they did not anticipate that Woolworth's white managers would—instead of threatening to have them arrested—flounder in confusion and embarrassment. The surprise discovery of defensiveness within the segregated white world turned their fear into elation.

In February 1960, four college students stage a lunch counter sit-in at a Woolworth's in Greensboro, North Carolina.

up the story. By the end of the week, the seventy-five-seat counter was filled with protesters, mostly students.

Spreading Protests

The demonstration quickly spread to Kress's, another downtown variety store. In addition to protesters at the lunch counters, dozens of picketers marched outside both stores to discourage shoppers from entering. Soon, many Greensboro stores and restaurants were posting signs to discourage potential protesters, such as "We Reserve the Right to Service the Public as We See Fit" and "CLOSED—In the Interest of Public Safety."[53]

The Greensboro protest immediately inspired activists elsewhere in the South. Within two weeks, similar sit-ins were under way in Virginia, South Carolina, Georgia, Florida, Alabama, and Tennessee. By April there were sit-ins in about eighty southern cities; an estimated fifty thousand protesters took part, and about two thousand of them were arrested. Northern branches of some chain stores with double standards were also picketed.

Protesters in Nashville, Tennessee, were especially well organized. The city's first sit-in, in mid-February, attracted around five hundred participants. For the next three months, Nashville experienced a continuous round of sit-ins in various public places.

"Jail, Not Bail"

All across the South, arrested protesters (who were usually charged with disorderly conduct) often countered with a technique called "jail, not bail." They claimed to be unable to pay bail or fines. This quickly filled the jails to capacity, drawing public attention and putting a financial burden on cities. Protesters kept jails full by immediately replacing one group with another. Activist Diane Nash recalled of one such protest:

> They said, "Everybody's under arrest." So all the students got up and marched to the wagon. Then they turned and looked around at the lunch counter again, and the second wave of students had all taken seats . . . then a third wave. No matter what they did and how many they arrested, there was still a lunch counter full of students there.[54]

Angry whites attack sit-in activists at a Mississippi lunch counter in 1963. Similar protests were staged throughout the South as news of the Greensboro sit-in spread.

Of course, this technique required constant supplies of new recruits. New faces were also needed because many dropped out as sit-ins dragged on for days and weeks. Some simply could not take enough time off from work or school. Others found prolonged humiliation and harassment from hostile whites unbearable.

Verbal abuse was the least of this harassment. Protesters had to endure eggs thrown at them, hot coffee or milk shakes poured down their backs, sugar and mustard dumped on their heads, and even cigarettes put out on their backs. Through it all, the protesters tried to remain calm. They avoided disruptive or violent reactions, wore good clothes, and remained quiet and respectful. Many read schoolbooks or Bibles. Often, they ended a day of silent protest with prayer.

SNCC

Some members of the black community, especially older ones, voiced concerns about the sit-in phenomenon. Protesters were scolded for putting themselves in danger, doing a disservice to their race, or creating a scandal. One student, John Lewis, recalled that his parents were "shocked and ashamed" when he was jailed:

"My mother made no distinction between being jailed for drunkenness and being jailed for demonstrating for civil rights."[55]

Such conflict was caused, in large part, by the youthfulness of the participants. Many of them were associated with a new group called the Student Nonviolent Coordinating Committee (SNCC, pronounced "snick"). Although committed to nonviolence, SNCC members were typically more aggressive than older activists, whom they saw as too conservative and afraid to take bold steps.

SNCC's aggressiveness and the popularity of sit-ins soon made it the dominant civil rights group in America. The youthful activists were responsible for expanding the civil rights battleground from courtrooms to direct public confrontations. Journalist Louis Lomax notes that this change was "proof that the Negro leadership class . . . was no longer the prime mover in the Negro's social revolt. [At the same time] the demonstrations . . . shifted the desegregation battles from the courtroom to the marketplace."[56]

A Crack in the Wall

As the sit-ins continued, stores that had been targeted began to suffer. White shoppers were wary of the turmoil, and black shoppers were not spending money there at all. The protests affected not only chains such as Woolworth and Kress but the economies of entire cities. The negative publicity that the sit-ins generated made it difficult for affected cities to attract new industry, trade, or conferences. And virtually every southern downtown felt the economic pinch. As one Nashville store owner commented, "You could roll a bowling ball down Church Street [a main downtown boulevard] and not hit anybody these days."[57]

Southern businessmen were therefore eager to end the protests. By spring the once-invulnerable wall of segregation began to crack, as the owners or managers of segregated stores began to relent. A turning point came when Nashville's mayor, Ben West, made a startling statement during a conference with sit-in leaders in April.

Activist Diane Nash asked West if he personally felt it was wrong for lunch counters to discriminate on the basis of color, and West said yes. The mayor recalled, "They asked me some pretty soul-searching questions. And one that was addressed to

"We Shall Overcome"

Shared songs were important to the civil rights movement. These "freedom songs" were sung in jail, while marching, or in other situations to help keep protesters' spirits up. Taylor Branch, in *Parting the Waters*, notes, "The spirit of the songs could sweep up the crowd, and the young leaders realized that through song they could induce humble people to say and feel things that otherwise were beyond them."

Some freedom songs were old, such as "Kumbaya," "Amazing Grace," and the movement's signature song, "We Shall Overcome." Many were adapted from gospel songs, reflecting the deep religious roots of the civil rights movement. Others were completely new songs, such as the angry protest songs written by the young folksinger Bob Dylan. Dylan's "Blowin' in the Wind" became one of the civil rights movement's most popular anthems.

In Juan Williams's *Eyes on the Prize*, civil rights activist and singer Bernice Johnson Reagon recalls, "They could not stop our sound. They would have had to kill us to stop us from singing. Sometimes the police would plead and say, 'Please stop singing.' And you would just know that your word was being heard, and you felt joy. There is a way in which those songs kept us from being touched by people who would not want us to be who we were becoming."

me as a man . . . was a moral question—one that a *man* had to answer, not a politician."[58]

Ending the Sit-Ins

The next day's newspapers blared the news that a prominent white politician did not oppose integrating lunch counters. Within a few weeks, six Nashville lunch counters began serving blacks, and (although some southern lunch counters did not desegregate for years) other cities followed suit.

The Greensboro Woolworth sit-in that had sparked the movement lasted until July 25, 1960, when the lunch counter there began serving African Americans. The four students who had launched the protest were not the first to eat there, however. Three of the counter's kitchen workers, surrounded by media and well-wishers, were given that honor. One of them, Geneva Tisdale, chose egg salad; she knew it would be good, Tisdale said, because she had made it herself earlier that day.

The success of the sit-in movement inspired variations across the South all through the early 1960s. There were wade-ins at pools and beaches, kneel-ins at churches, and stand-ins at ticket counters. At the same time, CORE activists began planning another major protest.

The Freedom Riders

This time they took on another powerful symbol of segregation: interstate transportation. The Supreme Court had ruled in 1960 that segregation in interstate transportation was illegal, giving all people the right to travel from state to state on public transport. However, the administration of President John F. Kennedy had been slow to enforce the ruling.

The protesters' plan was to force Kennedy into action by provoking segregationists, who had made it clear they would violently oppose enforcement. The hope was that the resulting publicity would dramatically show Kennedy—and the world—what was at stake. As CORE director James Farmer commented, "We felt we could count on the racists of the South to create a crisis so that the federal government would be compelled to enforce the law."[59]

The plan was to send a racially mixed group of volunteers, called freedom riders, on a bus trip through the South. In the spring of 1961, thirteen freedom riders—primarily students, though their ages ranged into the sixties—met for three days of planning and training in nonviolent tactics. They agreed to mix up the races on board the buses: Whites would sit in the back and blacks in the front, and at least one mixed pair would always sit together. At rest stops, they would use "white" and "colored" bathrooms opposite to their respective colors, and they would eat together at whites-only lunch counters.

The freedom riders left Washington, D.C., on May 4 in two groups, one on a Trailways bus and one on a Greyhound. They were bound for New Orleans, Louisiana, by way of Georgia, Alabama, and Mississippi. Branch wryly notes that they were heading into dangerous territory, far from the lofty ideals of integration and nonviolence: "Most of the bus stations [along the way] were located in parts of town where the Supreme Court and Gandhi were seldom discussed."[60]

Violence on the Road

Black communities along the way were ready to provide accommodations and other support. However, opponents of the freedom riders were also ready. The activists had anticipated that the most serious violence would come in Alabama, and they were right. There were few serious incidents until May 14, when an angry mob met one of the buses at the Anniston, Alabama, terminal. The bus's tires were slashed and some of its windows broken before the driver could drive away.

A few miles outside town, pursued by a caravan of cars, the bus slowed as its tires began to deflate. The driver pulled over and fled into a field as a group of angry whites surrounded the bus. The passengers tried to lock the doors and windows, but someone threw a firebomb through a broken window. The passengers, trying to escape the flames, found the exit doors blocked by the mob. Then a gas tank exploded and the mob moved back, allowing the protesters to escape.

Once outside, the freedom riders were attacked with lead pipes and baseball bats. Before anyone was killed, an undercover Alabama policeman who had been on board fired his gun into the air and held the mob back until state troopers arrived to disperse it. Eventually, a caravan of cars driven by protest supporters arrived to rescue the riders and take them to Birmingham.

The Other Bus

The second bus also encountered a violent mob in Anniston. This time, the driver was able to get the bus away without damage. He took back roads to Birmingham, hoping to avoid trouble. At the Birmingham terminal, however, the bus encountered a waiting mob and no police.

The city's police chief, Eugene "Bull" Connor, later claimed that he had posted no officers at the bus depot because it was a holiday, Mother's Day. Decades later, it was revealed that Connor had guaranteed the mob fifteen minutes before any officers

Freedom riders hang protest signs from the windows of their bus as they leave New York. When they arrived in Alabama, they were met by an angry white mob.

would arrive. The mob thus had plenty of time to attack the freedom riders without fear of being held back.

In the resulting violence, several protesters were beaten so badly that they required hospitalization. The injured were refused aid by one hospital that was afraid of reprisal, but they eventually found help elsewhere. Alabama's governor, John Patterson, commenting on the day's violence, offered no apologies: "When you go somewhere looking for trouble, you usually find it. . . . You just can't guarantee the safety of a fool and that's what these folks are, just fools."[61]

Another Try

The freedom riders reconvened, but their confidence in reaching their goal without serious casualties was shaken. They voted to fly to New Orleans. Bomb threats temporarily stopped flights on the Birmingham–New Orleans run, but they were eventually able to leave Alabama.

The freedom rides did not end there. Ten SNCC activists came from Nashville to Birmingham, determined to resume the abandoned journey to New Orleans. When their bus arrived in Birmingham, police forced anyone whose ticket showed travel between Nashville and New Orleans to stay on board. One activist escaped, however, because she had joined the group in Pulaski, Tennessee, and so had a different ticket.

She phoned a colleague in Nashville, who called the U.S. Justice Department. Within an hour, the protesters were allowed to leave the bus. However, they had to wait in the bus terminal overnight before a driver willing to take them could be found. As they waited, a line of policemen kept a mob estimated at three thousand away.

Once a driver was found, on May 20, the next leg of the trip, to Montgomery, was uneventful. However, at the Montgomery station, things grew eerily quiet. Then the police cars that had been providing protection suddenly disappeared and a crowd of

Just outside the town of Anniston, Alabama, a group of stunned freedom riders sits on the grass after a violent white mob firebombed their bus.

several hundred appeared. Freedom rider Frederick Leonard recalled, "All of a sudden, just like magic, white people everywhere. Sticks and bricks. [Cries of] 'Niggers. Kill the niggers'."[62]

The freedom riders were savagely beaten as reporters looked on helplessly. Several had to be hospitalized, including John Siegenthaler, the personal representative of President Kennedy's brother, Attorney General Robert Kennedy. Nonetheless, the riders remained determined. Jim Zwerg, a white protester who was among the most badly beaten, spoke for the group when he declared from his hospital bed, "We will continue our journey one way or another. We are prepared to die."[63]

Martin Luther King attended a mass meeting at a Montgomery church in support of the protesters. When a hostile crowd surrounded the building, the freedom riders and their supporters spent a night trapped in the church basement. Alabama's governor decided he could not maintain order and declared martial law. The next day, the protesters and their supporters were ferried out a few at a time in National Guard trucks.

On to Jackson

The situation was creating a furor; John and Robert Kennedy knew they had to act. Unwilling to allow more violence but wary of angering southern politicians, they brokered a deal. Under its terms, twelve protesters, sixteen reporters, and a dozen guardsmen traveled in a single bus to Jackson, Mississippi. To discourage ambushes, they were escorted by police motorcycles, cars, helicopters, and planes, a contingent so heavy that it was, according to Taylor Branch, "worthy of a NATO war game."[64]

In keeping with the deal, the group was arrested after arriving in Jackson and using the whites-only restrooms. Then the protesters created more pressure. In the next few days, more than 350 people descended on Jackson, allowing themselves to be arrested and refusing to pay bail.

Many were sent to a maximum-security Mississippi prison farm, where they served brutal six-month sentences that included bad food, beatings, and other hardships. Some of the punishments were petty humiliations; when the prisoners sang songs of freedom in their cells, for instance, guards took away their mattresses and blankets. Still, for the most part the prisoners managed to

"You Live in a Beautiful City"

As protests continued, many white authorities appealed to the black community for peace. In 1963 the mayor of Jackson, Mississippi, Allen Thompson, made a televised request. NAACP worker Medgar Evers responded in another televised message. Both are reprinted in Juan Williams's *Eyes on the Prize*.

Thompson: You live in a beautiful city. . . . You have twenty-four-hour protection by the police [and] the fire department [and a place where you can] make a comfortable living. . . . Now with these privileges . . . come certain responsibilities. . . . Do not listen to false rumors which will stir you, worry you and upset you. Refuse to pay attention to these outside agitators who . . . will advocate destroying everything that you and the white people working side by side [with you] have built up over the last hundred years.

Evers: [An African American in Jackson] looks about . . . and what does he see, to quote our mayor, in this "progressive, beautiful, friendly, prosperous city with an exciting future"? . . . He sees a city where Negro citizens are refused admittance to the city auditorium and the coliseum; his children refused a good ticket to a movie in a downtown theater; his wife and children refused service at a lunch counter in a downtown store. . . . He sees a city of over 150,000 of which forty percent is Negro, in which there is not a single Negro policeman or policewoman, school crossing guard, fireman, clerk, stenographer.

keep their spirits up, as when one rider, Hank Thomas, shouted, "Come get my mattress! I'll keep my soul!"[65]

What the Freedom Riders Accomplished

White segregationists had hoped that the brutal beatings and harsh prison sentences would crush the freedom riders. In a way, the plan succeeded. The activists never did complete their original journey. Many spent months in jail, and some victims of beatings suffered permanent physical injury.

On the other hand, the freedom riders succeeded brilliantly in alerting the nation to their message. The stark contrasts between the violent white mobs and the passively resistant activists were vividly depicted in newspapers and on TV around the world. At the same time, the Kennedy administration was forced to take a clear stand on civil rights.

As a direct result of the freedom rides, Kennedy directed the Interstate Commerce Commission to create and enforce regulations ending segregation in interstate bus travel. This ruling, more specific than the 1960 Supreme Court mandate, took effect in the fall of 1961, and even more sweeping changes were soon to come. The movement was about to enter its most active phase.

Chapter Five

Birmingham, Selma, and Washington, D.C.

There were more hard-won success stories for the movement in the early 1960s. One prominent example was the admittance of James Meredith as the first black student at the University of Mississippi (though federal troops were required to assure his continuing attendance). However, the movement also had some bitter setbacks. Notable was the SCLC's failure, after a year of hard work, to integrate the public facilities of Albany, Georgia. The *New York Herald Tribune* called the situation in Albany "a devastating loss of face."[66]

By the spring of 1963, dispirited activists were sorely in need of a victory. They chose to focus on Birmingham, Alabama, a place already so notorious for racial violence (including eighteen unsolved bombings in six years) that it was nicknamed "Bombingham." The city had become a potent symbol of southern segregation, and activists knew that a victory there would reverberate across the region. As SCLC worker Wyatt Walker commented, "We decided on Birmingham with the attitude that we may not win it, we may lose everything. But we knew that as Birmingham went, so went the South."[67]

Fire Hoses and Police Dogs

Part of the Birmingham campaign was a series of demonstrations that used only children and young adults. Activists chose this bold tactic because they believed that the sight of young people being arrested would be a dramatic signal to the nation. SCLC leaders also reasoned that adults might be reluctant to march out of fear of losing their jobs. James Bevel, who conceived the plan, commented, "A boy from high school has the same effect in terms of being in jail, in terms of putting pressure on the city, as his father, and yet there's no economic threat to the family, because the father is still on the job."[68]

The protesters—some as young as six, but mostly teenagers—first tried marching to City Hall on May 2. Before the marchers reached the downtown area, Bull Connor, the police commissioner, ordered them taken to jail for "safekeeping." Another group of protesters then appeared in their place, and another. Police had to use school buses to transport all of them. By day's end, nearly a thousand young people packed the city jail.

The next day, hundreds more, adults and teens, again tried to reach City Hall. This time, police used billy clubs, electric cattle

Police in Birmingham, Alabama, spray black demonstrators with fire hoses. The police attacks infuriated the American public and sympathy for the protesters heightened.

prods, and K-9 (dog) units to disperse them. City firefighters also used special water hoses. The spray was powerful enough to knock bricks from buildings and strip bark from trees. When turned on humans, it broke bones and knocked people down. Many ran, but those who stayed were blown down the street, according to Branch, "like scraps of refuse in a high wind."[69]

A Call for New Legislation

The vicious police tactics only served to increase public sympathy for the protesters. Images of white authorities attacking peaceful (and often young) black protesters made the front pages of newspapers around the world and virtually every news show in America. Sympathy for the protesters grew so strong that one activist remarked later that Bull Connor's police dogs and fire hoses deserved some of the credit for future civil rights gains.

President John F. Kennedy speaks in July 1963 about the violence in Alabama, promising sweeping civil rights legislation.

Birmingham's segregationist policies began to crumble. The business community, fearing potential riots, opened its lunch counters and hired more black workers. Bull Connor, increasingly seen as a brutal and outdated relic, was forced to step down. The Birmingham campaign also sparked a wave of nearly one thousand demonstrations elsewhere. Historian Adam Fairclough comments, "To list the places where black people engaged in nonviolent protests [after Birmingham] would be to name virtually every town and city in the South."[70]

Most important of all was the federal government's response. Until now, Kennedy had been reluctant to sponsor major civil rights legislation. After Birmingham, however, he proposed a sweeping new bill. Addressing Congress in June, Kennedy asked,

> If an American, because his skin is dark, cannot eat lunch in a restaurant open to the public; if he cannot send his children to the best public school available; if he cannot vote for the public officials who represent him; if, in short, he cannot enjoy the full and free life which all of us want, then who among us would be content to have the color of his skin changed and stand in his place? Who among us would then be content with the counsels of patience and delay?[71]

The March on Washington

Eager to demonstrate support for Kennedy's initiative, activists began organizing a massive new demonstration. This was the March on Washington, which brought an estimated 250,000 people to the nation's capital for the biggest nonviolent protest gathering in history. To many, the March on Washington was the finest moment in civil rights history, the highest expression of everything that the movement stood for.

The march, set for August 28, 1963, was organized in record time. Within weeks, thousands of pamphlets for potential group leaders were distributed nationwide. Local families and churches were urged to make room for visiting marchers. Public-address systems and portable toilets were located and installed. Police departments in D.C. and the surrounding suburbs underwent emergency crowd-control training. Bayard Rustin, a key organizer, recalled, "We wanted to get everybody from the whole country into Washington by nine o'clock in the morning and out of Washington by sundown. This required all kinds of things that you had to think through."[72]

Funding came from many sources, from the sale of buttons at 25 cents apiece to cash donations, large and small, from individuals and groups. Further support came from the public endorsement of a wide variety of celebrities. Among these were black entertainers such as musician Quincy Jones, singers Sammy Davis Jr. and Harry Belafonte, and actor Sidney Poitier. White celebrities, including singer Tony Bennett and actors Charlton Heston, Paul Newman, and Marlon Brando, also voiced their support.

The Masses Arrive

On the morning of the march, attendees poured into Washington. One observer estimated that at one point one hundred chartered buses were coming through the Baltimore Tunnel every hour. While most attendees came by plane, train, or bus, some arrived in less orthodox ways. A group of CORE members walked 230 miles from Brooklyn, New York. Others came by bicycle from as far away as South Dakota. One young man traveled from Chicago, nearly seven hundred miles away, on roller skates.

It was a mixed crowd. According to later estimates, about 15 percent were students and about one-quarter was white. Many of the black participants were middle-class northern urbanites, but the crowd included thousands of poor, rural blacks. The event took

Thousands gather in front of the Washington Monument during the August 1963 March on Washington when Martin Luther King Jr. delivered his famous "I have a dream" speech.

It Can't Happen Here

◼

The night of the aborted march from Selma to Montgomery, television stations nationwide interrupted their normal programming to broadcast film of the violence. ABC had been showing a documentary on Nazi war crimes, and many viewers—unable to believe that such brutality could happen in America—thought the clips of the Selma incident were simply part of the film. Journalist George Leonard noted (in his essay "Midnight Plane to Alabama: Journey of Conscience," in Carson et al.'s *The Eyes on the Prize Civil Rights Reader*), "With the cameras rather far removed from the action and the skies partly overcast everything that happened took on the quality of an old newsreel. Yet this very quality, vague and half silhouetted, gave the scene the vehemence and immediacy of a dream."

on a communal, optimistic atmosphere, and its sheer size was stunning. Taylor Branch comments: "The gathering sea of placards and faces produced the most brain-numbing sight since the first ghost fleet of empty buses chugged through Montgomery."[73]

"Free at Last!"

The day's program began with a speech by A. Philip Randolph. Randolph, the labor leader who had achieved job guarantees for blacks during World War II by threatening a similar march, was an appropriate choice as the opening speaker. Surveying the sea of people gathered at the Lincoln Memorial, he announced, "Fellow Americans . . . we are not a mob. We are the advance guard of a massive moral revolution."[74]

Randolph was followed by a wide variety of other speakers and performers. The latter included gospel singer Mahalia Jackson and opera star Marian Anderson. Folk singers Joan Baez, Odetta, Josh White, Bob Dylan, and Peter, Paul, and Mary—all strongly identified with the civil rights movement—also performed, leading the masses in stirring protest songs.

One of the many speakers was SNCC leader John Lewis, whose fiery speech reflected his organization's increasingly aggressive stance. Though he tempered his speech to placate older activists, the twenty-three-year-old Lewis's words were still powerful: "By the force of our demands, our determination, and our numbers, we shall splinter the segregated South into a thousand pieces, and put them back together in the image of God and democracy."[75]

However, the emotional highlight was Martin Luther King's closing speech, instantly famous and still considered one of the greatest examples of modern oratory. Inspired by the huge crowd's fervent response, King abandoned his four-minute prepared talk in favor of a semi-improvised, sixteen-minute flight of words. It ended with a stirring invocation of "that day when *all* God's children, black men and white men, Jews and Gentiles, Protestants and Catholics, will be able to join hands and sing in the words of the old Negro spiritual, 'Free at last! Free at last! Thank God Almighty, we are free at last!'"[76]

Four Dead in Birmingham

For civil rights leaders, the March on Washington was an undeniable triumph. They had organized, in record time, a huge gathering that made a powerful point but generated virtually no violence. Columnist Russell Baker noted in the *New York Times*, "No one could remember an invading army quite as gentle as the two hundred thousand civil-rights marchers who occupied Washington today. . . . The sweetness and patience of the crowd may have set some sort of national high-water mark in mass decency."[77]

For King, the day was a personal triumph as well, pushing him into the stratosphere of international prominence. He was named *Time* magazine's Man of the Year in 1964 and was awarded the 1964 Nobel Peace Prize. Regarding the Peace Prize, he was the youngest man, the second American, and only the third black man to receive this prestigious honor.

Nevertheless, the success of the march did little to lessen racial tension in the South, especially as the beginning of the school year neared. Once again, Alabama was a flashpoint in the struggle for integration, and its governor, George Wallace, vowed, "Segregation today. Segregation tomorrow. Segregation forever."[78] When Wallace tried to use the Alabama National Guard to block black students from entering Birmingham's public schools, President Kennedy federalized the troops and forced Wallace to comply.

Then, less than three weeks after the march, tragedy struck Birmingham. On Sunday, September 15, 1963, an explosion rocked the Sixteenth Street Baptist Church, which was full of children for a Youth Day celebration. Twenty-three people were injured and four were killed: Denise McNair, 11; Cynthia Wesley, 14; Carole Robertson, 14; and Addie May Collins, 14.

More than eight thousand mourners attended the somber funeral services for the four slain girls. Among them were Martin Luther King Jr. and hundreds of other religious leaders from around the country. No Birmingham city officials attended.

The Civil Rights Act

Two months later, on November 22, the nation experienced another, even more profound shock: the assassination of John F. Kennedy. It fell to his successor, Lyndon B. Johnson—a Texan and a pragmatic supporter of civil rights—to oversee in 1964 the passage of the legislation Kennedy had introduced.

This sweeping bill, the Civil Rights Act of 1964, was the strongest and farthest-reaching civil rights bill in history. It outlawed discrimination in all public facilities on the basis of race, color, religion, or national origin. (Public facilities, in this case, included businesses, such as restaurants and hotels, serving the general public.) The act also banned discrimination in employment, unions, and federal programs. Provisions were made to enforce the law through a variety of measures, such as threatening to withhold federal funds if states or organizations refused to comply.

Segregationists condemned the new legislation. Virginia congressman Howard Smith, for instance, called it "this monstrous instrument of oppression upon all the American people."[79] Johnson, however, hailed it as a crucial test for America's future: "My fellow citizens, we have come now to a time of testing. We must not fail. Let us close the springs of racial poison."[80]

"Lord Have Mercy on America"

The Civil Rights Act was a major step forward. However, it did little to remedy one deeply entrenched area of discrimination: voting rights. Activists knew that a solid voting bloc was a powerful tool for change. Although voting rights for black citizens

President Lyndon Johnson shakes hands with Martin Luther King Jr. after signing the 1964 Civil Rights Act, the strongest civil rights bill in American history.

had been established by the Fifteenth Amendment, the law was rarely enforced in southern states. King, commenting on the hollowness of the situation, remarked, "The Civil Rights Act of 1964 gave Negroes some part of their rightful dignity, but without the vote it was dignity without strength."[81]

Authorities had many ways to keep black voters from registering. For example, they intimidated would-be voters with threats of violence or job loss. Registrars' offices were also typically open at odd times, perhaps only twice a month for a few hours, to make registration difficult.

Another common tactic was to use unfair "literacy tests" designed to ensure that whites passed while even highly educated blacks failed. When one elderly farmer with a shaky hand asked for help in filling out the form, he was told he could not register if he could not write his address. The farmer replied, "I am 65 years old, I own 100 acres of land that is paid for, I am a taxpayer. . . . If what I done ain't good enough to be a registered voter with all the tax I got to pay, then Lord have mercy on America."[82]

Freedom Summer

Voting rights were especially restricted in Mississippi. Only a fraction of its eligible blacks were registered. Many whites insisted that this was simply because blacks did not want to vote. A bitter joke among activists about this attitude was "What has four eyes but can't see? Mississippi."

During the summer of 1964, several organizations banded together to send volunteers to Mississippi on a concerted registration drive called Freedom Summer. Field workers traveled all over the state, setting up educational workshops and talking with people about voting. Often, they also provided services such as health care and legal help to their poor, rural clients.

Predictably, the program met with violence. Medgar Evers, the NAACP's field director in Mississippi, had been murdered by a gunman the year before. Now, in 1964, houses were bombed, churches burned, and scores of people beaten or intimidated. The worst violence involved three young civil rights workers, Michael Schwerner, Andrew Goodman, and James Chaney, who disappeared after being jailed for speeding in Philadelphia, Mississippi.

A search was requested after they failed to check in with Freedom Summer headquarters, but the local sheriff refused, claiming that Schwerner, Goodman, and Chaney were hiding to generate publicity. Early in August, the bodies of the three men were found buried on a nearby farm. Nineteen men, including police officers, were indicted in the case; seven were convicted of a minor charge, that of interfering with the murdered trio's civil rights.

Bloody Sunday

More violence came in the spring of 1965. The SCLC was spearheading a voting-rights reform program in the small town of Selma, Alabama. During a demonstration, a young man named Jimmy Lee Jackson was shot and killed by police.

Saddened and outraged, activists turned the tragedy into a dramatic statement. In honor of Jackson, they decided to march fifty-four miles to the state capital of Montgomery. Albert Turner, a local activist, commented, "We . . . wanted to carry Jimmy's body to [Governor] George Wallace and dump it on the steps of the Capitol."[83]

Their first attempt, however, was a disaster. On what became known as Bloody Sunday, March 7, six hundred marchers were met by police and state troopers, some on horseback, on a bridge leading out of town. The police, firing tear gas and wielding clubs and whips, chased the marchers back across the bridge. At least fifty people required hospitalization. Sheyann Webb, who was eight when she marched, recalled, "People were turning and I saw this first part of the line running and stumbling back towards us . . . and somebody yelled, 'Oh, God, they're killing us!' I think I just froze then. There were people everywhere, jamming against me, pushing against me."[84]

"You Better Get Down There"

A second attempt at marching to Montgomery, to protest Jackson's death and to lobby for voter reform, began on March 21. This time, between 3,000 and 4,000 participants were protected by 1,800 federalized Alabama National Guardsmen, 2,000 army troops, 100 FBI agents, and 100 federal marshals. Selma's sheriff, Jim Clark, joked to reporters, "I'm glad to get rid of the ones that are leaving, but I wish they'd come back and get the rest of them."[85]

The protesters roughed it, marching sometimes in heavy rain, camping in tents, and relying on food brought in by supporters. As it progressed, the demonstration swelled dramatically; by the time it reached Montgomery, an estimated twenty-five thousand people, black and white, had joined in. Some were already heroes of the civil rights movement, such as Rosa Parks, Martin Luther King, and King's wife, Coretta Scott King. Others were celebrities in other ways, including comedian Dick Gregory and singers Harry Belafonte, Lena Horne, Sammy Davis Jr., Mahalia Jackson, Nina Simone, and Joan Baez.

By far, however, most of the marchers were ordinary people who simply wanted to show their support for voter reform. Journalist George Leonard recalls that, for him, it was a matter of conscience: "I had, of course, any number of reasons for not going to Selma, not the least of which was a powerful disinclination to be struck on the head and gassed. But as I raised that point and every other negative argument, a matter-of-fact voice answered: 'You better get down there.'"[86]

Alabama police attack civil rights protesters on Bloody Sunday in March 1965. A second protest began two weeks later in which celebrities and influential civil rights leaders participated.

It took five days for the protesters to reach Montgomery. For longtime activists, it was a triumphant return to the city where the bus boycott had signaled the movement's beginning a mere decade earlier. King capped the march by addressing a jubilant crowd from the steps of the state capitol building: "However difficult the moment, however frustrating the hour, it will not be long, because truth crushed to the earth will rise again. . . . How long? Not long. Because mine eyes have seen the glory of the coming of the Lord."[87]

The Voting Rights Act

The march from Selma was a success. It directly influenced the passage of still another important piece of federal legislation: the Voting Rights Act of 1965. This law finally outlawed racist tactics such as literacy tests, and gave federal officials the power to supervise registration if necessary. President Johnson called the bill "one of the most monumental laws in the entire history of American freedom" and added, "The vote is the most powerful instrument ever devised by man for breaking down injustice and destroying the terrible walls which imprison men because they are different from other men."[88]

"My Feets Is Tired"

Martin Luther King delivered a speech on the steps of the Montgomery capitol building after the march from Selma, invoking the words of an elderly parishioner of his church. The speech is reprinted in "Our God Is Marching On!" in Carson et al.'s *The Eyes on the Prize Civil Rights Reader.*

Our bodies are tired, and our feet are somewhat sore, but today as I stand before you and think back over that great march, I can say as Sister Pollard said, a seventy-year-old Negro woman who lived in this community during the bus boycott and one day she was asked while walking if she wanted a ride and when she answered, "No," the person said, "Well, aren't you tired?" And with her ungrammatical profundity, she said, "My feets is tired, but my soul is rested."

And in a real sense this afternoon, we can say that our feet are tired, but our souls are rested.

The Voting Rights Act had immediate results, creating a dramatic increase in black voters across the South. In 1964, 23 percent of voting-age blacks in America were registered. By 1969 that figure stood at 61 percent.

A number of other civil rights measures were also passed during this period. They included so-called affirmative action programs that gave minorities better opportunities in such areas as job promotions and scholarships. To Johnson, these laws simply made competition fairer. He stated, "You do not take a person who for years has been hobbled by chains and . . . bring him up to the starting line of a race, [saying] 'you are free to compete with all the others,' and still justly believe that you have been completely fair."[89]

Despite such measures, however, the pace of integration moved slowly. Dissension increased as many activists and ordinary blacks grew impatient with the movement's progress. Many of them were shifting to a path of increased militancy. The civil rights movement was about to fragment.

Chapter Six

Black Power Rises

By the late 1960s, the civil rights movement had achieved many significant gains. High school and college graduation figures for African Americans were rising sharply. More black Americans were buying houses and finding good jobs. And they had a much higher profile in the nation's arts, politics, and sports.

Nonetheless, the rate of change was far too slow for some. Statistics for violence, crime, drug use, and dependence on the welfare system within the black community were still dismayingly high. Income levels were still low; as of 1965, nearly one-half of black Americans lived below the poverty level. And blacks all over the country, not just in the South, still experienced discrimination, subtle or blatant, on a daily basis.

Simmering Tension

Activists, white and black, were not the only ones impatient with the rate of change. Many ordinary African Americans, especially young urban blacks, were increasingly frustrated as well. Their pent-up frustration built steadily and resulted in heightening racial tension. On occasion, this tension erupted into outright clashes. The most destructive of these took place in August 1965 in the Watts neighborhood of South Central Los Angeles, home to a majority of the city's black population.

The situation in Watts had long been volatile, for a number of reasons. Some involved conditions familiar to all urban blacks,

Businesses along a block in South Central Los Angeles lie in ruins after the August 1965 Watts Riots.

such as overcrowded and substandard housing, high unemployment and crime rates, poverty, and poor schools. Particular to Watts were allegations of violence and racial bias on the part of the all-white L.A. police force, as well as escalating tension between the neighborhood's mostly white shop owners and their customers. The summer of 1965 added still more factors, including a punishing heat wave and outrage over Proposition 14, a proposed state law that backers hoped would block the fair housing section of the Civil Rights Act.

A small incident—a routine traffic stop—was the spark that lit this tinderbox. A white policeman flagged down a young black man, Marquette Frye, on suspicion of drunk driving. Frye, who had indeed been drinking and driving erratically, tried to joke with the officer. Their loud, animated conversation attracted a crowd, and after onlookers began taunting the policeman, a second officer was called in.

"It Seemed Like Fun at First"

According to eyewitness accounts, one officer used his baton on a few people in the increasingly unruly crowd. Several were arrested in the fracas, including Frye and members of his family (who had been called to the scene by neighbors). News of the disturbance spread and the crowd swelled; when someone in the crowd broke a glass bottle, a full-scale riot began. What started as a spontaneous outburst against white authority quickly turned into widespread violence, looting, and burning. One participant recalled:

> It seemed like fun at first, throwing rocks at Whitey's big new cars. We didn't aim to hurt nobody, just mess up the cars. At least, not at first. Then it seemed like the stuff we took was just there for us. If we didn't take it, somebody else would. But then it got to be not so much fun at all, just trouble.[90]

An estimated thirty-five thousand people took part in the riot, which caused thirty-four deaths and about a thousand injuries and led to some three thousand arrests. Entire blocks were burned to the ground, with some two hundred businesses and one thousand buildings destroyed. Estimates for property damage ranged from $50 to $100 million. The damage was done almost exclusively to white-owned businesses and buildings; black churches, businesses, and homes were mostly left untouched. More that sixteen thousand National Guardsmen, county deputies, and city police intervened. After six days, the violence finally died down.

Long, Hot Summers

The Watts riot was only the most notorious of many disturbances of the period. Over the next four years, in what became widely known as "long, hot summers," racially motivated riots broke out across the country. The largest were in industrialized northern cities, including Newark, New Jersey, Chicago, Illinois, and Detroit, Michigan; but the violence crossed regional and size boundaries. Between 1966 and 1968 more than three hundred riots resulted in some two hundred deaths, the destruction of several thousand businesses, and hundreds of millions of dollars in property damage.

The chaos played a major role in the fracturing of the civil rights movement. Adding to this fragmentation were several dispiriting setbacks activists encountered in their attempts to organize peaceful demonstrations. The most prominent of these was in 1966, when the SCLC failed in its first attempt to desegregate the northern city of Chicago, one of the nation's largest and toughest cities.

The project, which focused on eliminating slum housing and opening white neighborhoods to blacks, was called the Chicago Freedom Movement. In Chicago, however, the SCLC's nonviolent methods, which had worked so well in the South, failed. King led a march to city hall on July 10, but rioting broke out two days later, and confrontations between marchers and so-called White Power mobs turned violent in July and August. King himself was hit with rocks while leading one demonstration. Chicago mayor Richard Daley, powerful head of the city's Democratic machine, met with King and publicly agreed that solutions were needed for the problem of urban slums, but did little to change the situation. Ultimately, the violence divided the black community and alienated many whites who might otherwise have been sympathetic to the movement.

Critics

In the face of this disappointment, and as incidents of rioting spread nationwide, many African Americans, especially young males, began rejecting the concept of nonviolent protest. More and more voiced harsh criticism of mainstream civil rights organizations such as the SCLC and NAACP, and of existing civil rights legislation, all of which they regarded as ineffective, old-fashioned, and insufficiently aggressive.

Increasingly, black activists criticized Martin Luther King. They complained that King and his colleagues often moved into situations where grassroots organizers had already been working hard and then took over, attracted media attention, and assumed the credit for victory. On one such occasion, Congressman Adam Clayton Powell scolded King for his actions following a riot in New York's Harlem neighborhood: "No leader outside of Harlem should come into this town and tell us what to do."[91]

Many began to feel that King's fame and importance to the movement was eclipsing other praiseworthy leaders and their

Congressman Adam Clayton Powell speaks to reporters in 1965. Powell was one of many activists who began criticizing Martin Luther King's tactics.

achievements. Two people often pointed out as examples were Robert Moses, the primary organizer of Freedom Summer, and Fannie Lou Hamer, who had played a crucial role in efforts to integrate the Mississippi Democratic Party during Freedom Summer.

Furthermore, many criticized King for expanding (and perhaps weakening) the focus on African American civil rights by speaking out against poverty in general and against the Vietnam War. King's critics complained that, by addressing so many issues at once, his effectiveness in the civil rights movement was compromised.

Black Is Beautiful

Meanwhile, a number of aggressive, militant philosophies and movements began to emerge as alternatives to established nonviolent forms of protest. Although each had distinctive characteristics, most of these can be loosely linked together under the heading of Black Power. The Black Power movement was essentially political, but it embraced much more. It was a broad philosophy

"The Blame Must Be Shared"

This excerpt from the influential 1967 book *Black Power*, by Stokely Carmichael and Charles Hamilton, reflects the disdain that young activists like Carmichael felt toward older, established advocates of nonviolence. The authors are speaking of the civil rights movement represented by Martin Luther King and the SCLC.

None of its so-called leaders could go into a rioting community and be listened to. In a sense, the blame must be shared—along with the mass media—by those leaders for what happened in Watts, Harlem, Chicago, Cleveland, and other places. Each time the black people in those cities saw Dr. Martin Luther King get slapped they became angry. When they saw little black girls bombed to death in a church and civil rights workers ambushed and murdered, they were angrier; and when nothing happened, they were steaming mad. We had nothing to offer that they could see, except to go out and be beaten again.

Stokely Carmichael speaks at a Mississippi rally. Carmichael advocated a philosophy of racial separatism.

of life that included everything from spiritual beliefs to historical research and fashion statements.

One important aspect of Black Power was a rejection (to varying degrees) of traditional white values. Under the banner of "Black is Beautiful," Black Power supporters popularized the idea that African Americans should not try to emulate typical white fashions. For example, instead of straightening one's hair, as was commonly the case then, styles such as Afro (or "natural") hair became fashionable. So did updated versions of traditional African clothing.

Black Power also sought to create a broad, renewed interest and pride in all aspects of the black community's culture. This included such topics as music, literature, history, and art. Black studies became an accepted course curriculum on many college campuses. In addition, black musical, dance, and theatrical groups were established in almost every U.S. city with a significant black population.

Many other aspects of daily life changed. The Black Power salute, an upraised fist, became a common sight. Also, part of the movement's push for respect and pride was the recognition that language plays a powerful role in daily life. As a result, there was a basic shift in terminology. Descriptive terms that had once been the accepted norms, such as *colored* and *Negro*, were now considered derogatory and replaced with terms still in use today, such as *black* and *African American*.

SNCC's Changes

The man probably most responsible for popularizing the term *Black Power* was a prominent young activist named Stokely Carmichael. When the fiery Carmichael was elected to the leadership of SNCC in 1966, it signaled a major shift in a group that had once been devoted to nonviolence.

Even before Carmichael's rise to power, SNCC was becoming noticeably more aggressive in its tactics. Under Carmichael, it instigated an overt philosophy of racial separatism. The organization rejected contact with the white establishment as much as possible. Carmichael encouraged the resignation of the organization's white staffers and volunteers. He also broke off relations with white financial supporters.

Carmichael's ideas were put forth in *Black Power*, an influential book he cowrote with Charles Hamilton in 1967. His ideas increasingly isolated him from many activists, black as well as white, and in 1969 he left America for Guinea, in Africa. His successor at SNCC, H. "Rap" Brown, maintained the group's separatist policies. Brown symbolized the group's new attitude by changing its name from Student Nonviolent Coordinating Committee to Student *National* Coordinating Committee.

Under Brown, the group's harsh views offended many people, and its base of supporters continued to disintegrate. Mainstream black civil rights groups had already severed their ties with the organization, and SNCC came close to bankruptcy as donations and membership plummeted. By the end of the 1960s it was no longer a viable organization.

The Panthers

As SNCC dissolved, another influential Black Power group was emerging. The Black Panther Party was founded in 1966 by student activists Huey Newton and Bobby Seale in Oakland, California. Its goal was to make the black community self-reliant so that it would not have to rely on the white establishment.

To this end, the Panthers organized services such as food and clothing banks, health clinics, and breakfast programs for children. These "survival programs" were familiar fixtures in black neighborhoods across the country in the late 1960s and early 1970s, as were the Panthers themselves in their distinctive black leather jackets, berets, and sunglasses.

The Panthers' survival programs were popular, beneficial, and often highly successful. However, the organization also espoused a belief that violence was justified to defend against what it considered widespread police brutality. This harsh attitude can be summed up in the group's embrace of Communist Chinese leader Mao Zedong's axiom "Power grows out of the barrel of a gun."[92]

Ordinary people and civil rights activists alike, white and black, were wary of the Panthers' violent and scornful attitudes. The Reverend Ralph Abernathy, one of the founders of the SCLC and an elder statesman of the movement, commented, "Those hard-eyed black boys had no respect for anything or anybody. To them a preacher was the next worse thing to a policeman, and religion was for old folks and suckers, both of whom they regarded with a fine contempt."[93]

Meanwhile, law enforcement agencies typically regarded the Panthers as little better than organized hoodlums, especially since the activists were suspected of organizing armed robberies to

What the Panthers Wanted

The Black Panther Party's official platform—its statement of intent—included ten demands. They are listed in the party's "Ten Point Plan."

1. We want freedom. We want power to determine the destiny of our black and oppressed communities.

2. We want full employment for our people.

3. We want an end to the robbery by the capitalists of our black and oppressed communities.

4. We want decent housing, fit for the shelter of human beings.

5. We want decent education for our people that exposes the true nature of this decadent American society. We want education that teaches us our true history and our role in the present-day society.

6. We want completely free health care for all black and oppressed people.

7. We want an immediate end to police brutality and murder of black people, other people of color, all oppressed people inside the United States.

8. We want an immediate end to all wars of aggression.

9. We want freedom for all black and oppressed people now held in U.S. federal, state, county, city and military prisons and jails. We want trials by a jury of peers for all persons charged with so-called crimes under the laws of this country.

10. We want land, bread, housing, education, clothing, justice, peace and people's community control of modern technology.

Members of the militant Black Panthers group protest in New York City in July 1968.

fund themselves. The group became a primary target for investigation by local police agencies and the FBI. In 1968 the FBI's director, J. Edgar Hoover, called the Panthers "the greatest threat to the internal security of our country."[94] (Hoover was antagonistic toward Martin Luther King as well, having ordered surveillance on him for years and referring to King as "the most dangerous Negro . . . in this nation."[95])

Malcolm X

Another fiery and influential black leader of the period was Malcolm X. (Born Malcolm Little, he rejected his "slave name.") Malcolm first came into the public eye as a prominent member of, and a primary spokesman for, the Nation of Islam, an organization also known as the Black Muslims.

Founded in the 1930s, the Nation of Islam drew some of its inspiration from mainstream Islam. It had a strong spiritual side, advocating success through personal discipline and religious piety. The group differed from mainstream Islam in many ways, however, notably in its emphasis on black pride and separatism. It taught that black people, over the centuries, had been systematically denied knowledge of their own past history and culture. The group's leaders also urged their followers to distance themselves from "white devils."

Like the Panthers, the Nation of Islam scorned mainstream civil rights organizations and their commitment to nonviolence. For example, Malcolm commented soon after the March on Washington, "The black masses are still without land, without jobs, and without homes. . . . Their Christian churches are still being bombed, their innocent little girls murdered. So what did the March on Washington accomplish? Nothing!"[96]

In 1963 the charismatic Malcolm, disillusioned with the leadership of the Nation of Islam, broke with the organization and founded his own group, the Organization of Afro-American Unity. He also began to temper his extreme views, advocating instead an urgent need for world brotherhood: "We must find a common approach, a common solution, to a common problem."[97] But his angry rhetoric, and the violence of the times, caught up with Malcolm. In 1965 he was assassinated at a speaking engagement in New York City, probably by three Black Muslim gunmen.

The Death of Dr. King

Terrible violence, including Malcolm's death, the armed resistance of the Panthers, and years of widespread rioting, continued to plague and divide the country. Then, in April 1968, came some of the most shocking violence yet: the assassination of Martin Luther King—the civil rights movement's most prominent leader, its most eloquent spokesman, and an icon of hope and faith for millions.

King's death occurred in Memphis, Tennessee, where he was helping organize striking members of the city's primarily black sanitation workers' union. King was scheduled to lead a march in support of the workers on April 4. That morning, however, the civil rights leader was standing on the balcony of the Lorraine Motel with two colleagues, Ralph Abernathy and Jesse Jackson, when a rifle shot felled him.

As news of King's death spread, a wave of grief engulfed the nation. Dozens of demonstrations, memorials, and rallies in his honor were held, including a march by an estimated forty thousand people in Memphis. In some cities public schools and libraries closed, as did museums, ports, businesses, and stock exchanges.

New York's governor, Nelson Rockefeller, ordered flags in front of public buildings to fly at half-staff. A number of major sporting events, the Academy Awards ceremony, and the presidential nomination campaigns were all postponed or suspended. Meanwhile, messages of condolence poured in from around the world. Typical was that of India's prime minister Indira Gandhi, who said, "Violence has removed one of the great men of the world."[98]

Within hours of Dr. King's death, President Lyndon Johnson made a televised speech. He told his audience,

> I know that every American of good will joins me in mourning the death of this outstanding leader and in praying for peace and understanding throughout this land. We can achieve nothing by lawlessness and divisiveness among the American people. It is only by joining together and only by working together that we can continue to move toward equality and fulfillment for all of our people. I hope that all Americans tonight will search their hearts as they ponder this most tragic incident.[99]

Martin Luther King Jr. lies bleeding to death on the balcony of a Memphis motel as friends point in the direction of the gunshot that struck him.

The Aftermath

A nationally televised memorial service was held on April 9 in Atlanta. Among those in attendance were former First Lady Jacqueline Kennedy, Vice President Hubert Humphrey, and Thurgood Marshall, now a U.S. Supreme Court justice. After the service, an estimated 100,000 mourners followed King's coffin to its burial place in Southview Cemetery.

Meanwhile, an international manhunt was underway to find the gunman. It resulted in the June arrest in London of an avowed white segregationist named James Earl Ray. Ray was tried and convicted of King's murder and sentenced to life in prison.

King's death had a number of immediate repercussions. Violent demonstrations broke out in several cities, most severely in New York, Chicago, Philadelphia, Baltimore, and Newark. In all, at least one hundred black communities across the nation were affected in some way or another by violence in the wake of King's murder.

"I've Seen the Promised Land"

Martin Luther King's last speech, before a crowd in Memphis the night before he was killed, was both inspirational and fatalistic. He discussed the bomb threat that had delayed his plane en route to Memphis and the time he had been stabbed by a deranged woman in a crowd. Unknowingly foreshadowing his imminent death, King concluded his speech with these words, reprinted in the *Eyes on the Prize Civil Rights Reader*, edited by Carson et al.

Well, I don't know what will happen now. We've got some difficult days ahead. But it doesn't matter with me now. Because I've been to the mountaintop. And I don't mind. Like anybody, I would like to live a long life. Longevity has its place. But I'm not concerned about that now. I just want to do God's will. And He's allowed me to go up to the mountain. And I've looked over. And I've seen the Promised Land. I may not get there with you. But I want you to know tonight, that we, as a people will get to the Promised Land. And I'm happy tonight. I'm not worried about anything. I'm not fearing any man. Mine eyes have seen the glory of the coming of the Lord.

Thousands of mourners march behind the casket during King's funeral procession.

In contrast, however, the shock of the event and the subsequent outpouring of grief nationwide had at least one immediate positive effect. It helped President Johnson persuade Congress to approve the Fair Housing Act of 1968. This legislation, the last major civil rights bill of the 1960s, prohibited racial discrimination in the sale or rental of most housing. Its passage helped put an end to repressive real estate practices that had often been used to keep black families from moving into predominantly white neighborhoods.

Never Recovering

The civil rights movement continued, but it never recovered from King's murder. No one person was able to match his fame, charisma, personal dignity, and political power. With no figurehead leader, and with increasing fragmentation of its agenda, the movement experienced a significant loss of momentum.

One example of this was the Poor People's Campaign, which King and his staff were planning at the time of his death. This was a tent city encampment on the National Mall in Washington, D.C., designed to call attention to poverty in America. The campaign did take place, under the auspices of the SCLC's new leader, Ralph Abernathy. However, the activists were not able to generate significant interest in Washington for new antipoverty legislation.

Several other factors helped stall the movement for black equality. Many activists chose to concentrate their efforts on protesting the Vietnam War. Also, Richard Nixon, who became president in 1969, was not a strong supporter of civil rights. Further slowing the process was the increasing disarray of the Black Panthers; by the 1970s, beset by legal problems, internal conflict, and concerted law enforcement efforts to cripple it, the group ceased to be a significant force. Nonetheless, despite these slowdowns, the civil rights movement kept moving into the 1970s and beyond.

Epilogue

The Dream
Lives On

In the decades following King's death, African Americans, in theory, had all the rights of other citizens. However, the dream of equality had not been realized. There was widespread feeling within the black community, for example, that America's law enforcement and judicial systems were inherently racist, and that huge inequalities in such areas as jobs, housing, and education still existed.

Furthermore, the sense of a unified movement was gone. A once-cohesive group had splintered into separate groups. Nonetheless, the accomplishments of the movement's key years were clear.

Office Holders

One of the most obvious accomplishments was in voting, as registration figures continued to rise. By 1976, 63 percent of eligible black voters were registered, only five percentage points below that for whites. As activists had hoped, these increases led to a steady number of blacks in office.

For example, in 1966 Edward Brooke became the first black senator since Reconstruction. In 1969 Shirley Chisholm became the first black female member of Congress. (She was also the first black woman to make a presidential bid on a major ticket. The

Reverend Jesse Jackson, an SCLC activist and a prominent civil rights leader, later also mounted two presidential bids on a major ticket.) In Georgia, John Lewis and Julian Bond were elected to the U.S. Congress and the state legislature, respectively.

Many black mayors were elected, including in Los Angeles (Tom Bradley), Atlanta (Maynard Jackson), Detroit (Coleman Young), and Washington, D.C. (Walter Washington). By the 1990s, America had a black governor (L. Douglas Wilder of Virginia) and a black female senator (Carol Moseley Braun). These were only a few examples; by the mid-1990s, blacks held about 8,000 of the roughly 500,000 elective offices in the nation.

At the same time, they were making inroads in other high political positions. In 1966 Robert C. Weaver became the first black cabinet member (secretary of Housing and Urban Development), and in 1967 civil rights lawyer Thurgood Marshall was appointed the first black Supreme Court justice. In the 1970s, President Jimmy Carter, a southerner, named Andrew Young the first black U.S. ambassador to the United Nations and Patricia Roberts Harris the first black woman cabinet member (secretary of housing and urban development). By the time Colin Powell and Condoleezza Rice were named successive secretaries of state under George W. Bush, African American politicians at the cabinet level were not unusual.

MLK Day

Another legacy of the civil rights era is the degree to which America honors that period. For instance, millions every year visit the National Civil Rights Museum in Memphis. Also, ceremonies regularly mark important occasions.

The most important of these is Martin Luther King Day, the third Monday in January (his birthday is January 15), which honors King with memorials and events all over the country. After much debate and considerable delay, President Ronald Reagan declared this a national holiday in 1983. (The holiday did not go into effect until 1986.) Even then, however, a day to honor King's memory was controversial; the governor of Arizona, for example, refused for years to recognize the holiday in his state.

Coretta Scott King, the slain leader's widow, remains the primary standard-bearer for her late husband's memory, speaking

Making It Official

◼

In November 1983 President Ronald Reagan announced that Martin Luther King Day would become an official national holiday. This excerpt from his speech is reproduced in Alex Ayres' *The Wisdom of Martin Luther King, Jr.*

> Dr. King's was truly a prophetic voice that reached out over the chasms of hostility, prejudice, ignorance, and fear to touch the conscience of America. He challenged us to make real the promise of America as a land of freedom, equality, opportunity, and brotherhood.
>
> The majesty of his message, the dignity of his bearing, and the righteousness of his cause are a lasting legacy. In a few short years he changed America for all time. He made it possible for our nation to move closer to the ideals set forth in our Declaration of Independence: that all people are created equal and are endowed with inalienable rights that government has the duty to respect and protect.

The Lorraine motel where Martin Luther King Jr. was assassinated in 1968 today has a museum that honors the civil rights leader's legacy.

often to public groups. Typical of her comments is this: "The day that Negro people and others in bondage are truly free, on the day 'want' is abolished, on the day wars are no more, on that day I know my husband will rest in a long-deserved peace."[100]

Justice Delayed

Activists also honor the memory of the movement by reopening old criminal cases in an attempt to find justice for victims of long-ago violence. One example involved Byron de la Beckwith, who was arrested after the murder of Mississippi NAACP leader Medgar Evers in 1963 but freed after two trials ended in hung juries. In 1994 de la Beckwith was tried and convicted on new evidence that he had boasted of the killing; he died while serving a life sentence.

Similarly, the case of the deadly 1963 bombing of the Birmingham church was reopened years later. The FBI had identified four men at the time as being responsible, but FBI director Hoover blocked prosecution and the case was closed. After it was reopened, three of the

Not a Foregone Conclusion

—————————◼—————————

Historian Adam Fairclough, in this excerpt from his book *Better Day Coming*, points out that today the segregation that existed in the South seems almost beyond belief, but in the 1960s integration did not seem to be a foregone conclusion.

> White supremacy, as a formal system, collapsed with such suddenness between 1963 and 1965 that one is tempted to conclude in hindsight that Jim Crow was a social, economic, and political anachronism, and that the Civil Rights Movement was pushing against an open door. . . . In retrospect, it seems almost incredible that the United States should have tolerated a regional version of apartheid as late as the 1960s. Yet before 1963 the triumph of the Civil Rights Movement did not look at all inevitable. It was far from obvious that nonviolent protests had the capability of transforming the South.

four—Robert Chambliss, Thomas Blanton Jr., and Bobby Frank Cherry—were sentenced to life in prison. The fourth, Herman Frank Cash, died before a case could be established against him.

James Earl Ray, Martin Luther King's confessed killer, recanted soon after his conviction. Some members of King's family supported Ray's appeal for a new trial. Tennessee authorities refused to reopen the case, however, and Ray died in 1998. Allegations of cover-ups continue to surface.

Though there were many suspects, no one was ever convicted in the 1964 murders of Schwerner, Chaney, and Goodman, the three voting-rights workers in Mississippi. However, the case was reopened after forty years. In January 2005 Baptist preacher Edgar Ray Killen, long suspected as the mastermind of the murders, was arrested and charged with the crime based on secretly taped and recently revealed incriminating testimony.

Challenges for the Future

For present-day activists, it is not enough to honor past achievements or punish past crimes. It is also crucial to secure the future by addressing ongoing controversies. One focus is the issue of affirmative action, the policy of increasing minority representation in higher education and business by allocating jobs and school admission slots to underrepresented groups, sometimes by quotas. Affirmative action programs were mandated in the 1960s to remedy past race discrimination, but charges of reverse discrimination led to Supreme Court decisions since the late 1990s that limited or abolished race- or sex-based preferences. Debate over what constitutes fair and necessary steps to increase black representation continues.

Another challenge is the always-present threat of racial violence. The worst example in recent years came in 1992, when rioting again broke out in Los Angeles. As before, the disturbance was sparked by a police confrontation; several white officers were accused of beating a black motorist named Rodney King, and although the beating was videotaped, the police were acquitted. In the violence that followed, fifty-three people died and about twenty-four hundred were injured, with over $1 billion in property damage. (Four officers were later indicted on lesser charges of violating King's civil rights, and two were convicted.)

In the period between the 1954 *Brown* decision and the death of Dr. King in 1968, nonviolent protest both altered history and transformed a race. Juan Williams comments, "Black people who had lived under oppression for 300 years gained a new sense of dignity and power and a truer sense of citizenship. White people were changed as well—after an unquestioned acceptance of a segregated society, many examined how they treated their black neighbors and went on to accept civil rights as human rights."[101] Those key years are gone, but the legacy of the civil rights movement continues.

Notes

Introduction: We Shall Overcome

1. Quoted in Juan Williams, *Eyes on the Prize: America's Civil Rights Years, 1954–1965.* New York: Viking, 1987, p. 35.
2. Quoted in Taylor Branch, *Parting the Waters: America in the King Years, 1954–63.* New York: Touchstone/Simon & Schuster, 1989, p. 195.
3. Martin Luther King Jr., "The American Dream," speech given in Atlanta, GA, July 4, 1965, MLK Papers Project. www.stanford.edu/group/King/publications/sermons/650704_The_American_Dream.html.
4. Quoted in Williams, *Eyes on the Prize*, p. 224.

Chapter 1: The Roots of the Civil Rights Movement

5. Quoted in Clayborne Carson, ed., *Civil Rights Chronicle: The African-American Struggle for Freedom.* Lincolnwood, IL: Legacy, 2003, p. 15.
6. Quoted in PBS, "Nat Turner's Rebellion," *Africans in America.* www.pbs.org/wgbh/aia/part3/3p1518.html.
7. Quoted in PBS, "John Brown," *Africans in America.* www.pbs.org/wgbh/aia/part4/4p1550.html.
8. Quoted in Nick Treanor, ed., *The Civil Rights Movement.* San Diego: Greenhaven, 2003, p. 33.

9. Quoted in Adam Fairclough, *Better Day Coming: Blacks and Equality, 1890–2000.* New York: Viking, 2001, p. 48.
10. Williams, *Eyes on the Prize*, p. 10.
11. Vincent Harding, "Prologue: We the People," in Clayborne Carson, David J. Garrow, Gerald Gill, Vincent Harding, and Darlene Clark Hine, eds., *The Eyes on the Prize Civil Rights Reader: Documents, Speeches, and Firsthand Accounts from the Black Freedom Struggle.* New York: Penguin, 1991, p. 5.
12. Quoted in Fairclough, *Better Day Coming*, p. 102.
13. Quoted in Fairclough, *Better Day Coming*, p. 186.

Chapter 2: Postwar Progress

14. Gould Beech, "Schools for a Minority," *Survey Graphic*, October 1939. http://newdeal.feri.org/survey/39b15.htm.
15. Quoted in *Houston Informer*, "Segregation Stories Nearing Climax," April 8, 1950, *Sweatt v. Painter.* Archive. www.law.du.edu/russell/lh/sweatt/inf/HI-040850.html.
16. Quoted in *Sweatt v. Painter*, 339 U.S. 629 (1950), *Sweatt v. Painter* Archive. www.law.du.edu/russell/lh/sweatt/docs/sweatt_ussc.html.

17. Quoted in *Austin American*, "South in Turmoil over *Sweatt* Rule," June 6, 1950, *Sweatt v. Painter* Archive. www.law.du.edu/russell/lh/sweatt/as/as060650a.html.

18. Quoted in *Austin American*, "South in Turmoil over *Sweatt* Rule."

19. Williams, *Eyes on the Prize*, p. 17.

20. Quoted in *McLaurin v. Oklahoma State Regents*, 339 U.S. 637 (1950), http://afroamhistory.about.com/library/blmclaurin_v_oklahoma.htm.

21. Williams, *Eyes on the Prize*, p. 21.

22. Quoted in Lisa Cozzens, "Early Civil Rights Struggles: *Brown v. Board of Education*," 1995. www.watson.org/~lisa/blackhistory/early-civilrights/brown.html.

23. Quoted in Juan Williams, *Thurgood Marshall: American Revolutionary*. New York: Times Books, 1998, p. 216.

24. Quoted in Carson, *Civil Rights Chronicle*, pp. 108–109.

25. Quoted in Fairclough, *Better Day Coming*, p. 220.

26. Quoted in Williams, *Eyes on the Prize*, p. 35.

27. Quoted in Williams, *Eyes on the Prize*, p. 34.

28. Quoted in Carson, *Civil Rights Chronicle*, p. 106.

29. Williams, *Eyes on the Prize*, p. 44.

30. Quoted in Carson, *Civil Rights Chronicle*, p. 96.

31. Henry Aaron, "Jackie Robinson," *Time 100*, June 14, 1999. www.time.com/time/time100/heroes/profile/robinson01.html.

Chapter 3: Victories in Montgomery and Little Rock

32. Quoted in Carson, *Civil Rights Chronicle*, p. 138.

33. Quoted in Branch, *Parting the Waters*, p. 131.

34. Branch, *Parting the Waters*, p. 135.

35. Quoted in Fairclough, *Better Day Coming*, p. 230.

36. Quoted in Williams, *Eyes on the Prize*, p. 77.

37. Quoted in Fairclough, *Better Day Coming*, p. 233.

38. Quoted in Carson, *Civil Rights Chronicle*, p. 154.

39. Quoted in Williams, *Eyes on the Prize*, p. 108.

40. Quoted in Lisa Cozzens, "School Integration in Little Rock, Arkansas: Background," 1998. www.watson.org/~lisa/blackhistory/school-integration/lilrock/backgnd.html.

41. Quoted in Williams, *Eyes on the Prize*, p. 100.

42. Daisy Bates, "The Long Shadow of Little Rock," in Carson et al., *The Eyes on the Prize Civil Rights Reader*, p. 98.

43. Quoted in Carson, *Civil Rights Chronicle*, p. 156.

44. Quoted in Lisa Cozzens, "The Little Rock Nine Enter Central High," 1998. www.watson.org/~lisa/blackhistory/school-integration/lilrock/9enter.html.

45. Quoted in Carson, *Civil Rights Chronicle*, p. 155.

46. Quoted in Williams, *Eyes on the Prize*, p. 110.
47. Branch, *Parting the Waters*, p. 223.
48. Quoted in Carson, *Civil Rights Chronicle*, p. 159.
49. Quoted in Williams, *Eyes on the Prize*, p. 118.
50. Quoted in Lisa Cozzens, "Public Schools Shut Down," 1998. www.watson.org/~lisa/blackhistory/school-integration/lilrock/shutdown.html.

Chapter 4: Sit-Ins and Freedom Rides

51. Quoted in Branch, *Parting the Waters*, p. 271.
52. Quoted in "Interview with Franklin McCain," in Carson et al., *The Eyes on the Prize Civil Rights Reader*, p. 115.
53. Quoted in Williams, *Eyes on the Prize*, p. 127.
54. Quoted in Carson, *Civil Rights Chronicle*, p. 182.
55. Quoted in Fairclough, *Better Day Coming*, p. 243.
56. Quoted in Lisa Cozzens, "Sit-Ins," 1997. www.watson.org/~lisa/blackhistory/civilrights-55-65/sit-ins.html.
57. Quoted in Williams, *Eyes on the Prize*, p. 135.
58. Quoted in Williams, *Eyes on the Prize*, p. 139.
59. Quoted in Williams, *Eyes on the Prize*, p. 147.
60. Branch, *Parting the Waters*, p. 413.
61. Quoted in Lisa Cozzens, "Freedom Rides," 1997. www.watson.org/~lisa/blackhistory/civilrights-55-65/freeride.html.
62. Quoted in Williams, *Eyes on the Prize*, p. 153.
63. Quoted in Branch, *Parting the Waters*, p. 450.
64. Branch, *Parting the Waters*, p. 470.
65. Quoted in Branch, *Parting the Waters*, p. 484.

Chapter 5: Birmingham, Selma, and Washington, D.C.

66. Quoted in Branch, *Parting the Waters*, p. 557.
67. Quoted in Fairclough, *Better Day Coming*, p. 274.
68. Quoted in Williams, *Eyes on the Prize*, p. 189.
69. Branch, *Parting the Waters*, p. 759.
70. Fairclough, *Better Day Coming*, p. 274.
71. Quoted in Theodore C. Sorensen, ed., *"Let the Word Go Forth": The Speeches, Statements, and Writings of John F. Kennedy, 1947–1963*. New York: Dell, 1988, p. 194.
72. Quoted in Williams, *Eyes on the Prize*, p. 198.
73. Branch, *Parting the Waters*, p. 878.
74. A. Philip Randolph, March on Washington address, 1963, White House Historical Association. www.whitehousehistory.org/04/subs/activities_03/d04_01.html.
75. Quoted in Mosi Secret, "March on Washington Revisited," *Village Voice*, August 27–September 2,

2003. www.villagevoice.com/issues/0335/secret.php.

76. Quoted in Branch, *Parting the Waters*, pp. 882–83.

77. Quoted in AfricanAmericans.com, "The March on Washington, 1963: 'We Stood on a Height.'" www.africanamericans.com./NewLeaders.htm.

78. Quoted in Fairclough, *Better Day Coming*, p. 289.

79. Quoted in Taylor Branch, *Pillar of Fire: America in the King Years, 1963–65*. New York: Simon & Schuster, 1998, pp. 388–89.

80. Quoted in Branch, *Pillar of Fire*, pp. 388–89.

81. Martin Luther King Jr., "Our God Is Marching On!" in Carson et al., *Eyes on the Prize Civil Rights Reader*, p. 224.

82. Quoted in Williams, *Eyes on the Prize*, p. 254.

83. Quoted in Williams, *Eyes on the Prize*, p. 267.

84. Quoted in Carson, *Civil Rights Chronicle*, p. 281.

85. Quoted in Williams, *Eyes on the Prize*, p. 282.

86. George B. Leonard, "Midnight Plane to Alabama: Journey of Conscience," in Carson, *The Eyes on the Prize Civil Rights Reader*, p. 214.

87. Quoted in Lisa Cozzens, "Mississippi and Freedom Summer," 1997. www.watson.org/~lisa/blackhistory/civilrights-55-65/mississippi.html.

88. Quoted in Williams, *Eyes on the Prize*, p. 285.

89. Quoted in Treanor, *The Civil Rights Movement*, p. 28.

Chapter 6: Black Power Rises

90. Quoted in Elizabeth A. Wheeler, "More than the Western Sky: Watts on Television, August 1965," *Journal of Film and Video*, July 2003. http://elibrary.bigchalk.com/libweb/elib/do/document?set=search&groupid=1&requestid=lib_standard&resultid=8&edition=&ts=4F82732D4FA5DCC94A14A459EBAFD5DF_1104437296204&urn=urn%3Abigchalk%3AUS%3BBCLib%3Bd.

91. Quoted in Branch, *Pillar of Fire*, p. 447.

92. Quoted in Fairclough, *Better Day Coming*, p. 317.

93. Quoted in Fairclough, *Better Day Coming*, p. 301.

94. Quoted in the Church Committee Report, "The FBI's Efforts to Disrupt and Neutralize the Black Panther Party," in Carson et al., *The Eyes on the Prize Civil Rights Reader*, p. 529.

95. Quoted in Branch, *Pillar of Fire*, p. 150.

96. Quoted in James H. Cone, *Martin and Malcolm and America: A Dream or a Nightmare*. Maryknoll, NY: Orbis, 1991, p. 113.

97. Quoted in Cone, *Martin and Malcolm and America*, p. 193.

98. Quoted in Australian Associated Press, "Assassination Stuns U.S., World Leaders," *Age*, April 6, 1968. http://150.theage.com.au/view_best

ofarticle.asp?straction=update&int type=1&intid=960.

99. Lyndon B. Johnson, "Statement by the President on the Assassination of Dr. Martin Luther King, Jr.," April 4, 1968, American Presidency Project. www.presidency.ucsb.edu/ws/index.php?pid=28781&st=&st1=.

Epilogue: The Dream Lives On

100. Quoted in Carson, *Civil Rights Chronicle*, p. 346.
101. Williams, *Eyes on the Prize*, p. 287.

Chronology

1863 The Emancipation Proclamation abolishes slavery in the Confederate states and allows the Union army to recruit black soldiers for the first time.

1865 The Thirteenth Amendment to the Constitution is ratified, outlawing slavery in all areas of the United States.

1866 The Ku Klux Klan, a secret organization designed to intimidate and victimize blacks, is founded in Pulaski, Tennessee.

1868 The Fourteenth Amendment confers citizenship on all persons born or naturalized in the United States, thereby extending citizenship to blacks, and guarantees citizens due process and equal protection under the law.

1870 The Fifteenth Amendment guarantees all citizens the right to vote without regard to race or previous condition of slavery.

1896 In *Plessy v. Ferguson*, the Supreme Court rules that "separate but equal" facilities do not violate Fourteenth Amendment guarantees; this gives legal sanction to segregationist Jim Crow laws.

1909 The National Association for the Advancement of Colored People (NAACP) is founded.

1917 The United States enters World War I; some 370,000 black Americans will serve in the U.S. military by the war's end in November 1918.

1918–1930 Approximately 1 million blacks migrate from the American South to northern cities in search of jobs and better living conditions.

1941 America enters World War II; under pressure from black union leaders, President Franklin D. Roosevelt issues an executive order forbidding discrimination in defense industries.

1947 Jackie Robinson becomes the first African American to play Major League Baseball in the twentieth century.

1948 President Harry Truman orders full desegregation of the armed forces.

1950 The NAACP wins two landmark Supreme Court cases involving segregation in public higher education, *Sweatt v. Painter* and *McLaurin v. Oklahoma*.

1954 In *Brown v. Board of Education of Topeka, Kansas*, the Supreme Court overturns school segregation laws.

1955 Rosa Parks refuses to change seats on a bus in Montgomery, Alabama, setting off a yearlong boycott of the city's bus system. The boycott ends with the Supreme Court's outlawing segregation on public transportation. It also marks the emergence of Martin Luther King Jr. as a civil rights leader.

1957 The Southern Christian Leadership Conference, a coalition of civil rights and religious leaders, is founded, with King its first president. Little Rock, Arkansas's Central High School is forcibly integrated.

1960 The Student Nonviolent Coordinating Committee (SNCC), soon to be a leader in civil rights protest, is founded.

1961 The freedom rides, protests designed to test integration on interstate bus transportation, end in serious violence.

1962 James Meredith becomes the first black student at the University of Mississippi.

1963 The March on Washington occurs. President John F. Kennedy orders the National Guard to stand by as the University of Alabama is desegregated.

1964 During the volatile Freedom Summer voting-rights program in Mississippi, the murder of three activists ignites nationwide protest. President Lyndon B. Johnson signs the Civil Rights Act. King accepts the Nobel Peace Prize.

1965 Activist Malcolm X is murdered. King leads a massive march from Selma to Montgomery, calling attention to the need for voter registration in Alabama. The Voting Rights Act passes. The destructive and deadly Watts riots erupt in the summer.

1965–1968 Widespread urban riots, marked by arson, looting, and police violence, mar a series of "long, hot summers."

1966 Influential militant group the Black Panther Party is founded. SNCC leader Stokely Carmichael popularizes the phrase "Black Power," which comes to represent a new attitude of confrontation. The SCLC fails in its push to integrate public facilities in Chicago.

1967 NAACP lawyer Thurgood Marshall becomes the first black Supreme Court justice.

1968 Martin Luther King is assassinated in Memphis, Tennessee. Grieving and angry black communities across the country respond with memorial services and, in some cases, rioting.

1983 Martin Luther King Day is declared a national holiday.

For Further Reading

Books

Sara Bullard, *Free at Last: A History of the Civil Rights Movement and Those Who Died in the Struggle*. New York: Oxford University Press, 1993. This book chronicles the movement, year by year, in clear prose and excellent photos. Among the highlights are profiles of many neglected victims and heroes of the struggle for civil rights.

John M. Dunn, *The Civil Rights Movement*. San Diego: Lucent, 1998. A volume in Lucent's World History series, this thorough history includes significant people, events, speeches, and background.

Harvey Fireside, *The "Mississippi Burning" Civil Rights Murder Conspiracy Trial*. Berkeley Heights, NJ: Enslow, 2002. This well-written book, part of the Headline Court Case series, examines the murders of three civil rights activists in 1964 and the difficulty of prosecuting the case.

Charles George, *Civil Rights: The Struggle for Black Equality*. San Diego: Lucent, 2001. This book focuses on how words such as speeches and legal documents shaped the civil rights movement.

James Haskins, *Freedom Rides: Journey for Justice*. New York: Hyperion Books for Children, 1995. A well-written account of a crucial part of the civil rights movement.

Pierre Hauser, *Great Ambitions*. New York: Chelsea House, 1995. This book, part of the Milestones in Black American History series, covers the years 1896 to 1909.

Eileen Lucas, *Civil Rights: The Long Struggle*. Springfield, NJ: Enslow, 1996. A part of the series Issues in Focus, this book takes a broader look at the history of civil rights.

Fred Powledge, *We Shall Overcome: Heroes of the Civil Rights Movement*. New York: Scribner's, 1993. This series of clear, short biographies, focusing on nonfamous people, was written by a former reporter who covered the civil rights movement.

Nigel Ritchie, *Lives in Crisis: The Civil Rights Movement*. Hauppage, NY: Barron's, 2002. A well-illustrated introduction to the movement.

Flip Schulke, *He Had a Dream: Martin Luther King, Jr., and the Civil Rights Movement*. New York: W.W. Norton, 1995. A book of black-and-white photos and brief commentary by a photojournalist who extensively covered the movement. Though the text is not specifically for young readers, these striking (and sometimes frightening) photos provide an excellent background to the story.

Joyce Carol Thomas, ed., *Linda Brown, You Are Not Alone: The* Brown v. Board of Education *Decision*. New York: Jump at the Sun/Hyperion Books for Children, 2003. An interesting collection of poems, stories, and personal reflections focused on the epic school desegregation case.

Michael Weber, *Causes and Consequences of the African American Civil Rights Movement*. Austin, TX: Raintree Steck-Vaughn, 1998. A well-written look at the movement, along with the events that led up to it, and its legacy.

Web Sites

African American History. This is an extensive site maintained by Lisa Cozzens while a student at Brown University. Links include detailed discussions of key events from 1955–1965. www.watson.org/~lisa/black history/index.html.

Civil Rights: Law and History (www.usdoj.gov/kidspage/crt/crtmenu.htm). A bare-bones but very informative site maintained as part of the U.S. Department of Justice's Kids and Youth Page.

In Pursuit of Freedom and Equality: *Brown v. Board of Education of Topeka* (http://brownvboard.org). An excellent and detailed site dedicated to the landmark Court decision, maintained by the nonprofit Brown Foundation.

Martin Luther King Jr. and the Civil Rights Movement (http://seattle-times.nwsource.com/mlk). An excellent resource of photos and essays, maintained by a division of the *Seattle Times*.

National Urban League. "About Us—History," The history of this civil rights organization established in 1910. www.nul.org/about/history.htm.

Sweatt v. Painter Archive "U.S. Supreme Court Opinion," maintained by the Denver University School of Law. www.law.du.edu/russell/lh/sweatt.

Works Consulted

Books

Alex Ayres, ed., *The Wisdom of Martin Luther King. Jr.* Cleveland, Meridian, 1993. Some of the most famous and inspirational of King's public speeches and essays are presented here, along with other material such as Ronald Reagan's speech naming Martin Luther King Day a national holiday.

Taylor Branch, *Parting the Waters: America in the King Years, 1954–63.* New York: Touchstone/Simon & Schuster, 1989. This masterly mixture of history and biography won the Pulitzer Prize.

———, *Pillar of Fire: America in the King Years, 1963–65.* New York: Simon & Schuster, 1998. The second in Branch's projected epic trilogy.

Stokely Carmichael and Charles Hamilton, *Black Power: The Politics of Liberation in America.* New York: Vintage, 1992. A reprint of an influential 1967 book coauthored by Carmichael, then a leading young civil rights activist.

Clayborne Carson, ed., *Civil Rights Chronicle: The African-American Struggle for Freedom.* Lincolnwood, IL: Legacy, 2003. This well-illustrated, large-format book provides a good overview.

Clayborne Carson, David J. Garrow, Gerald Gill, Vincent Harding, and Darlene Clark Hine, eds., *The Eyes on the Prize Civil Rights Reader: Documents, Speech-es, and Firsthand Accounts from the Black Freedom Struggle.* New York: Penguin, 1991. An excellent compendium of documents, essays, and other material from the era.

James H. Cone, *Martin and Malcolm and America: A Dream or a Nightmare.* Maryknoll, NY: Orbis, 1991. This book focuses on two charismatic leaders, King and Malcolm X, as a way of exploring America in the 1960s.

Adam Fairclough, *Better Day Coming: Blacks and Equality, 1890–2000.* New York: Viking, 2001. Fairclough is a British historian, and his book provides an interesting and different take on the civil rights movement.

Kay Mills, *This Little Light of Mine: The Life of Fannie Lou Hamer.* New York: Flume Penguin, 1993. A biography of the distinguished civil rights worker from Mississippi.

Theodore C. Sorensen, ed., *"Let the Word Go Forth": The Speeches, Statements, and Writings of John F. Kennedy, 1947–1963.* New York: Dell, 1988. Sorensen, a historian and Kennedy expert, edited the late president's speeches and writings.

Nick Treanor, ed., *The Civil Rights Movement.* San Diego: Greenhaven, 2003. Part of the American Social Movements series, this book includes excerpts from crucial writings and speeches of the era.

Juan Williams, *Eyes on the Prize: America's Civil Rights Years, 1954–1965*. New York: Viking, 1987. This excellent book cogently and concisely presents a wealth of material.

———, *Thurgood Marshall: American Revolutionary*. New York: Times Books, 1998. A biography of the influential NAACP lawyer and Supreme Court justice.

Periodicals
Jennifer Sullivan, "Widow of Civil-Rights Activist Blames Mississippi Officials," *Seattle Times*, January 9, 2005.

Internet Sources
Henry Aaron, "Jackie Robinson," *Time 100*, June 14, 1999. www.time.com/time/time100/heroes/profile/robinson01.html.

AfricanAmericans.com, "The March on Washington, 1963: 'We Stood on a Height.'" www.africanamericans.com/NewLeaders.htm.

Austin American, "South in Turmoil over *Sweatt* Rule," June 6, 1950, *Sweatt v. Painter* Archive. www.law.du.edu/russell/lh/sweatt/as/as060650a.html.

Australian Associated Press, "Assassination Stuns U.S., World Leaders," *Age*, April 6, 1968. http://150.theage.com.au/view_bestofarticle.asp?straction=update&inttype=1&intid=960.

Gould Beech, "Schools for a Minority," *Survey Graphic*, October 1939. http://newdeal.feri.org/survey/39b15.htm.

Black Panther Party, "The Ten Point Plans." www.blackpanther.org/TenPoint.htm.

Brown Quarterly, "Teacher Talk: A Lesson Plan About Eleanor Roosevelt," Winter 2002. http://brownvboard.org/brwnqurt/05-1/05-1f.htm.

Lisa Cozzens, "Early Civil Rights Struggles: *Brown v. Board of Education*," 1995. www.watson.org/~lisa/blackhistory/early-civilrights/brown.html.

———, "Freedom Rides," 1997. www.watson.org/~lisa/blackhistory/civilrights-55-65/freeride.html.

———, "The Little Rock Nine Enter Central High," 1998. www.watson.org/~lisa/blackhistory/school-integration/lilrock/9enter.html.

———, "Mississippi and Freedom Summer," 1997. www.watson.org/~lisa/blackhistory/civilrights-55-65/missippi.html.

———, "Public Schools Shut Down," 1998. www.watson.org/~lisa/blackhistory/school-integration/lilrock/shutdown.html.

———, "School Integration in Little Rock, Arkansas: Background," 1998. www.watson.org/~lisa/blackhistory/school-integration/lilrock/backgnd.html.

———, "Sit-Ins," 1997. www.watson.org/~lisa/blackhistory/civilrights-55-65/sit-ins.html.

Houston Informer, "Segregation Stories Hearing Climax," April 8, 1950, *Sweatt v. Painter* Archive. www.law.du.edu/russell/lh/sweatt/inf/HI-040850.html.

Lyndon B. Johnson, "Statement by the President on the Assassination of Dr. Martin Luther King, Jr.," April 4, 1968, American Presidency Project. www.presidency.ucsb.edu/ws/index.php?pid=28781&st=&st1=.

Martin Luther King Jr., "The American Dream," speech given in Atlanta, GA, July 4, 1965, MLK Papers Project. www.stanford.edu/group/king/publications/sermons/650704-The-American-Dream.html.

"King's Assassination (4 April 1968)," MLK Papers Project, 2002. www.stanford.edu/group/King/about-king/encyclopedia/king-assassination.htm.

McLaurin v. Oklahoma State Regents, 339 U.S. 637 (1950). http://afroamhistory.about.com/library/blmclaurin_v_oklahoma.htm.

PBS, "John Brown," *Africans in America*. www.pbs.org/wgbh/aia/part4/4p1550.html.

———, "Nat Turner's Rebellion," *Africans in America*. www.pbs.org/wgbh/aia/part3/3p1518.html.

A. Philip Randolph, March on Washington address, 1963, White House Historical Association. www.whitehousehistory.org/04/subs/activities_03/d04_01.html.

Mosi Secret, "March on Washington Revisited," *Village Voice*, August 27–September 2, 2003. www.villagevoice.com/issues/0335/secret.php.

Swann v. Mecklenburg, U.S. Supreme Court 402 U.S. 1, April 20, 1971, Legal Information Institute, http:// supct.law.cornell.edu/supct/search/ind ex.html.

Sweatt v. Painter, 339 U.S. 629 (1950), *Sweatt v. Painter* Archive. www.law.du/edu/russell/lh/sweatt/docs/sweatt_ussc.html.

Elizabeth A. Wheeler, "More than the Western Sky: Watts on Television, August 1965," *Journal of Film and Video*, July 2003. http://elibrary.bigchalk.com/libweb/elib/do/document?set=search&groupid=1&requestid=lib-standard&resul-tid=8&edition=&ts=4F82732D4FAS-DCC94A14A459EBAFD5DF-1104437296204&urn=urn%3Abigchalk%3AUS%3BBCLib%3Bd

"White and Opposition Reaction," letter in *Montgomery Advertiser*, January 13, 1956, Montgomery Homepage. http://home.att.net/~renigua/whiteandopposition.html.

William Yeingst, "Sitting for Justice," *Increase & Diffusion* magazine. www.si.edu/i%2bd/sitins.arc.html.

Index

Picture Credits

Cover: © Flip Schulke/CORBIS

© Bettmann/CORBIS, 8, 17, 19 (both), 22, 31, 34, 50, 52, 57, 63, 66, 73, 76, 79, 83, 87

© CORBIS, 64

© Kevin Fleming/CORBIS, 91

Library of Congress, 3, 6, 11, 19 (left), 24, 25 (both), 33, 35, 37, 48, 58, 62, 75, 79

North Wind Picture Archive, 14

Schomberg Center for Research into Black Culture, 7, 28

Time-Life Pictures/Getty Images, 38, 44, 46, 86

About the Author

Adam Woog has written more than forty books for adults, teens, and children. For Lucent Books, he has explored such subjects as Louis Armstrong, the Elizabethan theater, Prohibition, Anne Frank, Elvis Presley, sweatshops, and the New Deal. Woog lives with his wife and their daughter in Seattle, Washington.